STAMP DECORATING

STAMP DECORATING

Transform your home in minutes with the simplest new decorating technique

STEWART & SALLY WALTON

PHOTOGRAPHY BY GRAHAM RAE

LORENZ BOOKS

NEW YORK • LONDON • SYDNEY • BATH

This edition published in 1996 by Lorenz Books,
an imprint of Anness Publishing Inc,
27 West 20th Street, New York 10011

Lorenz Books are available for bulk purchase, for sales promotion
and for premium use. For details, write or call the manager of special sales,
LORENZ BOOKS, 27 West 20th Street, New York, NY 10011;
(212) 807-6739

Produced by Anness Publishing Limited
Hermes House, 88-89 Blackfriars Road, London SE1 8HA

ISBN 1-85967-306-6

Publisher: Joanna Lorenz
Senior editor: Lindsay Porter
Project editor: Sarah Ainley
Photographer: Graham Rae
Designer: Bobbie Colgate Stone
Stylists: Diana Civil, Andrea Spencer and Fanny Ward

Printed and bound in Hong Kong

CONTENTS

ℐNTRODUCTION

EVERY NOW AND THEN THERE IS A BREAKTHROUGH IN INTERIOR DECORATING — SOMETHING NEW CAPTURES

THE IMAGINATION. STAMPING IS DEFINITELY ONE SUCH BREAKTHROUGH — IT IS ONE OF THE MOST INSTANT AND

INNOVATIVE DECORATING TECHNIQUES AVAILABLE. WONDERFULLY SIMPLE YET STUNNINGLY EFFECTIVE, STAMPED

DESIGNS CAN BE USED TO TRANSFORM ANYTHING FROM ENTIRE WALLS TO SHEETS OF GIFTWRAP; TO CREATE A

THEME FOR A WHOLE ROOM OR TO PROVIDE ORIGINAL ACCESSORIES FOR AN EYE-CATCHING DISPLAY.

THE STAMP DECORATING IDEA COMES FROM THE RUBBER OFFICE STAMP AND IT USES THE SAME PRINCIPLE —

ALL THE EQUIPMENT YOU WILL NEED IS A STAMP AND SOME COLOR. COMMERCIAL STAMPS ARE READILY

AVAILABLE, BUT INCLUDED IN THIS BOOK IS PRACTICAL ADVICE ON HOW TO CREATE YOUR OWN STAMPS FROM

WOOD OR SPONGE, RUBBER OR LINOLEUM — ALMOST ANY MATERIAL THAT WILL HOLD COLOR AND RELEASE IT.

STAMPS CAN BE USED WITH AN INK PAD, BUT A SMALL FOAM ROLLER GIVES A BETTER EFFECT: JUST COAT THE STAMP

WITH INK OR ORDINARY HOUSEHOLD PAINT — THIS MAKES STAMPING A FAIRLY INEXPENSIVE OPTION AND GIVES

YOU A WIDE RANGE OF COLORS TO CHOOSE FROM. FOLLOW THE TIPS ON APPLICATION TECHNIQUES AND

PAINT EFFECTS TO ACHIEVE THE LOOK BEST SUITED TO YOUR HOME.

OVER 40 STYLISH DECORATING IDEAS ARE FEATURED IN THIS BOOK, BEAUTIFULLY PHOTOGRAPHED WITH CLEAR

STEP-BY-STEP INSTRUCTIONS. YOU ARE SURE TO PROGRESS ON TO YOUR OWN PROJECTS ONCE YOU HAVE

MASTERED THE BASIC TECHNIQUES — TRANSFORMING INTERIORS HAS NEVER BEEN SO TEMPTINGLY EASY.

CREATING STAMPS

WOOD AND LINOLEUM

Stamped prints were first made with carved wooden blocks. Indian textiles are still produced by hand in this way and it has recently become possible to buy traditional carved printing blocks.

Designs are cut in outline and the backgrounds are scooped out to leave the pattern shapes standing free of the surface. Ink is applied, either by dipping the block or rolling color on to the surface. The design is stamped and appears in reverse. The craft of making wooden printing blocks takes time to learn: you need special tools that are razor sharp, and an understanding about cutting with or against the grain. Practice on a bonded wood like marine-grade plywood, which is relatively easy to carve.

Linoleum blocks are available from art and craft suppliers and usually come ready mounted in a range of sizes. Linoleum is a natural material made from ground cork and linseed oil on a webbed string backing. It is cut in the same way as wood, but has a less resistant texture and no grain to contend with.

To make a linoleum stamp you will need to trace a design and reverse the tracing before transferring it; this way you will print the design the right way around. Fill in all the background areas with a permanent marker pen: these are the parts to be scooped out, leaving the design free of the surface. You will need a minimum of three tools - a scalpel, a V-shaped nib and a U-shaped nib. All the tools should be kept sharp to make cutting safer. Linoleum is easiest to cut when a bit warm, so place the block on a radiator for ten minutes before cutting. Hold the block with your spare hand behind your cutting hand, so if the tool slips you will not hurt yourself.

FOAM STAMPS

Different types of foam are characterized by their density. The main types used for stamp-making in this book are: high-density foam rubber, such as upholstery foam rubber; medium-density sponge, such as a kitchen sponge; and low-density sponge, such as a bath sponge. The different densities are each suited to a particular kind of project; on the whole, medium- or low-density sponges are best for bold solid shapes, and high-density foam rubber for fine details. Polystyrene can also be used but must be mounted on to composition board. When the glue has dried, the polystyrene can be cut through to the

▲ *Create the effect of wood blocks (top) with handmade linoleum blocks (bottom).*

There are two methods of creating your own rubber stamps. The first is to design on paper and then have a rubber-stamp company make one for you. This is worth doing if you intend to make good use of the stamp, and not just use it for a small, one-time project. Custom-made stamps are quite expensive to produce, so unless money is no object you may like to consider a second option. You can also make stamps by carving your design into an ordinary eraser. Many erasers are now made of a plastic compound instead of actual rubber, but the surface is smooth and easy to cut into. There are two projects in this book, the tea set and personalized stationery, that show you how to transfer and cut a pattern, and then print from a homemade rubber stamp.

▲ *Homemade stamps cut from foam rubber and sponge.*

▼ *Commercial rubber stamps are available in designs to suit all tastes.*

board and the background can be lifted, leaving the design as a stamp.

To make a sponge stamp, first trace your chosen design then lightly spray the back of the pattern with adhesive, which will make it tacky but removable. Stick the pattern on the sponge and use a sharp scalpel to cut around the shape. Remove any background by cutting across to meet the outlines. If you are using medium- or low-density sponge part it after the initial outline cut, then cut right through to the other side. High-density foam rubber can be cut into and carved out in finer detail, it is also less absorbent, so you get a smoother, less textured print. If you are stamping over a large area, it is easier to mount the foam on to a composition board base and use wood glue to attach a small wooden door knob to the back, as a handle.

RUBBER STAMPS

Rubber stamps have come out of the office and playroom and emerged as remarkable interior decorating tools. Stores have sprung up dealing exclusively in an incredible range of stamp designs and the mail-order selections are astounding. The advantage of these pre-cut stamps is that you are instantly ready to transform fabric, furniture, even walls - and there can be no quicker way to add pattern to a surface. However, rubber stamps are most suited to small projects that require fine detail.

CREATING STAMPS

JACOBEAN POLYSTYRENE FLOWER

Polystyrene is easy to cut and gives good, clean edges. Always mount the polystyrene on composition board before you cut your pattern.

YOU WILL NEED
- ◆ *sheet of polystyrene, approximately ½in thick*
- ◆ *piece of composition board, the same size as the polystyrene*
- ◆ *wood glue or white glue*
- ◆ *felt-tipped pen*
- ◆ *scalpel*

1 Stick the sheet of polystyrene and composition board backing together with wood glue or white glue.

2 Without waiting for the glue to set, draw the design using a felt-tipped pen. Remember that the pattern will reverse when printed.

3 Cut around the outline of the design using a scalpel. If this is done before the glue has set, these pieces will pull away easily.

4 Cut the edging details, removing unwanted pieces as you go.

5 Make shallow, angular cuts and scoop out the pattern details of the design. Use a new blade for this so that the cuts are sharp and you do not accidentally lift adjoining particles that have been only partially separated.

GEOMETRIC BORDER DESIGN

This border stamp is made from high-density foam rubber. A good quality upholstery foam rubber is recommended. The piece used here was sold by a camping supply shop for use as a portable, compact mattress.

YOU WILL NEED
- *high-density foam rubber, such as upholstery foam*
- *composition board, cut to the same size*
- *wood glue or white glue*
- *felt-tipped pen*
- *ruler*
- *scalpel*
- *wooden block, for the handle*

1 Stick the foam rubber on to the composition board by applying wood glue or white glue to the rough side.

2 Without waiting for the glue to set, draw the pattern on to the foam rubber using a felt-tipped pen and ruler. Use a scalpel to outline the sections to be cut away, then lift them out. If the glue is still tacky, this will be much easier.

3 Finally, using wood glue or white glue, stick the wooden block in the middle of the stamp back, to act as a handle. Allow to dry thoroughly.

SQUIGGLE FOAM RUBBER STAMP

Foam rubber comes in all shapes, sizes and densities. Make a visit to a specialized dealer, as inspiration for new ideas often springs from the discovery of new materials. Here is an idea for making a squiggle stamp in an original way.

YOU WILL NEED
- *masking tape*
- *length of cylindrical foam rubber about ¾in in diameter*
- *wood glue or white glue*
- *composition board*

1 Lay out a length of masking tape, sticky side up. Twist the foam rubber into a squiggle shape, pressing it on to the middle section of the tape.

2 Apply wood glue or white glue to the untaped side of the foam rubber and turn it face-down on to the composition board. Fold the tape ends under the board to hold the foam rubber in place while the glue sets. When dry, peel off the masking tape.

FLORAL LINOCUT

Cutting lino is a simple technique to master. You will be delighted with the intricacy of the motifs you can create using this medium.

YOU WILL NEED
- ♦ *tracing paper*
- ♦ *pencil*
- ♦ *sheet of transfer paper*
- ♦ *lino block*
- ♦ *masking tape*
- ♦ *scalpel*
- ♦ *lino-cutting tools: a "V"-shaped gouge and a "U"-shaped scoop*

1 Make a tracing of your chosen motif, the same size as the lino block. Slip a sheet of transfer paper (chalky side down) between the tracing and the lino, then tape the edges with masking tape.

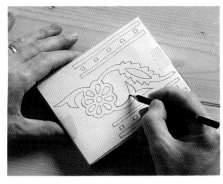

2 Draw over the pattern lines with a sharp pencil. The tracing will appear on the lino block.

3 Remove the paper and cut around the outline with a scalpel. Cut any fine detail or straight lines by making shallow, angular cuts from each side, then scoop out the "V"-shaped sections.

4 Cut the rest of the pattern using the lino tools - the scoop for removing large areas of background, and the gouge for cutting the finer curves and pattern details. Hold the lino down firmly, with your spare hand placed behind your cutting hand to avoid accidents.

POTATO PRINT SUNBURST

Most of us learn the technique of using potatoes for printing as very young schoolchildren. Potato prints are amazingly effective, and should not be overlooked by adults.

————————————

YOU WILL NEED
♦ *medium-sized raw potato*
♦ *sharp kitchen knife*
♦ *fine felt-tipped pen*
♦ *scalpel*

1 Use a kitchen knife to make a single cut right through the potato. This will give the smoothest surface.

2 Draw the motif on to the potato with a fine felt-tipped pen. Remember that motifs reverse when stamped, although with the sunburst motif used here it will make no difference.

3 Use a scalpel to cut the outline, then undercut and scoop out the background. Potato stamps will not last longer than a few hours before they deteriorate, so keep a tracing of your motif if your project cannot be completed in one go. The design can then be re-cut using a fresh potato.

BASIC APPLICATION TECHNIQUES

Stamping is a simple and direct way of making a print. The variations come from the way in which the stamp is inked and the type of surface to which it is applied. The stamps used in the projects were inked with a foam roller which is easy to do and gives reliable results, but each application technique has its own character. It is a good idea to experiment to find the method and effect that you most prefer.

INKING WITH A BRUSH
The advantage of this technique is that you can see where the color has been applied. This method is quite time consuming, so use it for smaller projects. It is ideal for inking an intricate stamp with more than one color.

INKING WITH A FOAM ROLLER
This is the very best method for stamping large areas such as walls. The stamp is evenly inked, and you can see where the color has been applied. Variations in the clarity of the prints can be achieved by re-inking the stamp after several printings.

INKING ON A STAMP PAD
This is the traditional way to ink rubber stamps, which are less porous than foam rollers. The method is suitable for small projects, particularly printing on paper. Stamp pads are more expensive to use than paint but are less messy and will produce very sharp prints.

INKING BY DIPPING IN PAINT
Spread a thin layer of paint onto a flat plate and dip the stamp into it This is the quickest way of stamping large decorating projects. Since you cannot see how much paint the stamp is picking up, you will need to experiment first.

INKING WITH FABRIC PAINT
Spread a thin layer of fabric paint onto a flat plate and dip the stamp into it. Fabric paints are quite sticky and any excess paint is more likely to be taken up in the fabric rather than to spread around the edges. Fabric paint can also be applied by brush or foam roller, and is available with built-in applicators from special outlets.

INKING WITH SEVERAL COLORS
A brush is the preferred option when using more than one color on a stamp. It allows greater accuracy than a foam roller because you can see exactly where you are putting the color. Two-color stamping is very effective for giving a shadow effect or a decorative pattern.

SURFACE APPLICATIONS

The surface on to which you stamp your design will greatly influence the finished effect.
Below are just some of the effects that can be achieved.

STAMPING ON ROUGH PLASTER

You can roughen your walls before stamping by mixing joint compound to a fairly loose consistency and spreading it randomly on the wall. When dry, roughen with coarse sandpaper, using random strokes.

STAMPING ON SMOOTH PLASTER OR WALLPAPER LINER

Ink the stamp with a small foam roller for the crispest print. You can create perfect repetitions by re-inking with every print, whereas making several prints between inkings varies the density of the prints and is more in keeping with hand printing.

STAMPING ON WOOD

Rub down the surface of any wood to give the paint a better "tooth" to adhere to. Some woods are very porous and absorb paint. Intensify the color by stamping over the print later. If you stamp wood lightly the grain will show through. Seal your design with clear matte varnish.

STAMPING ON GLASS

Wash glass in hot water and detergent to remove any dirt or grease and dry thoroughly. It is best to stamp on glass not used for food, such as vases. Ink the stamp with a foam roller and practise on a spare sheet of glass. As glass has a slippery, non porous surface, you need to apply the stamp with a direct on/off movement. Each print will have a slightly different character, and the glass's transparency will allow the pattern to be viewed from all sides.

STAMPING ON TILES

Wash and dry glazed tiles thoroughly before stamping. If the tiles are already on the wall, avoid stamping in areas that require a lot of cleaning. The stamps will only withstand a gentle wipe with a damp cloth. Loose tiles can be baked to add strength and permanence to the paint. Read the paint manufacturer's instructions (and disclaimers!) before you do this. Ink the stamp with a small foam roller and apply with a direct on/off movement.

STAMPING ON FABRIC

As a rule, natural fabrics are the most absorbent, but to judge the stamped effect, experiment on a small sample. Fabric paints come in a range of colors, but to obtain subtler shades you may need to combine the primaries with black or white. Always place a sheet of cardboard behind the fabric to protect your work surface. Apply the fabric paint with a foam roller, brush or by dipping. You will need more paint than for a wall surface, as fabric absorbs more paint.

PAINT EFFECTS

Once you have mastered the basics of stamp decorating, there are other techniques you can use to enrich the patterns and add variety. Stamped patterns can be glazed over or overprinted to inject subtle or dramatic character changes.

STAMPING LATEX PAINT ON PLASTER, DISTRESSED WITH TINTED VARNISH

The stamped pattern will already have picked up the irregularities of the wall surface and, if you re-ink after several prints, some prints will look more faded than others. To give the appearance of old hand-blocked wallpaper, paint over the whole surface with a ready-mixed antiquing varnish. You can also add color to a varnish, but never mix a water-based product with an oil-based one.

STAMPING LATEX PAINT ON PLASTER, COLORED WITH TINTED VARNISH

If the stamped prints have dried to a brighter or duller shade than you had hoped for, you can apply a coat of colored varnish to modify the tone. It is possible to buy ready-mixed color-tinted varnish, or you can add color to a clear varnish base. A blue tint changes red into purple, a red changes yellow into orange, and so on. The color changes are gentle because the background changes at the same time.

STAMPING WITH WALLPAPER PASTE, WHITE GLUE AND WATERCOLOR PAINT

Mix three parts pre-mixed wallpaper paste with one part white glue and add watercolors. These come ready-mixed in bottles with internal droppers. The colors are intense, so you may only need a few drops. The combination gives a sticky substance which the stamp picks up well and which clings to the wall without drips. The white glue dries clear to give a bright, glazed finish.

STAMPING WITH A MIXTURE OF WALLPAPER PASTE AND LATEX PAINT

Mix up some wallpaper paste and add one part to two parts latex paint. This mixture makes a thicker print that is less opaque than the usual latex paint version. It also leaves a glazed surface that picks up the light.

STAMPING LATEX PAINT ON PLASTER, WITH A SHADOW EFFECT

Applying even pressure gives a flat print. By pressing down more firmly on one side of the stamp than on the other, you can create a shadow effect on one edge. This is most effective if you repeat the procedure, placing the emphasis on the same side each time.

STAMPING A DROPPED SHADOW EFFECT

To make a pattern appear three-dimensional, stamp each pattern twice. Make the first print in a dark color that shows up well against a mid-tone background. For the second print, move the stamp slightly to one side and use a lighter color.

DESIGNING WITH STAMPS

To design a pattern with stamps, you need to achieve a compromise between printing totally at random and measuring precisely with machine-like regularity. To obtain effective results, you can use the stamp block itself as a means of measuring your pattern, or try strips of paper, squares of cardboard and lengths of string. Try using a stamp pad on scrap paper to plan your design, but always wash and dry the stamp before proceeding to the main event.

USING PAPER CUTOUTS
The easiest way to plan your design is to stamp and cut out as many pattern elements as you need and use them to mark the position of your finished stamped prints.

CREATING A REPEAT PATTERN
Use a strip of paper as a measuring device for repeat patterns. Cut the strip the length of one row of the pattern. Use the stamp block to mark where each print will go, with equal spaces in between. To space the rows, mark up a vertical strip and position the horizontal strip against it to print.

USING A PAPER SPACING DEVICE
This method is very simple. Decide on the distance between prints and cut a strip of paper to that size. Each time you stamp, place the strip against the edge of the previous print and line up the edge of the block with the other side of the strip. Or use a longer strip to measure the total distance required.

CREATING AN IRREGULAR PATTERN
If your design doesn't fit into a regular grid, plan it first on paper. Cut out paper shapes to represent the spaces between the stamps and use these to position the finished pattern. Alternatively, raise a motif above the previous one by stamping above a strip of card positioned on the baseline.

DEVISING A LARGER MOTIF
Use the stamps in groups to make up a larger design. Try stamping four together in a block, or partially overlapping an edge so that only a section of the stamp is shown. Use the stamps upside down, back to back and rotated in different ways. Experiment on scrap paper first.

USING A PLUMB LINE
Attach a plumb line at ceiling height to hang down the wall. Hold a cardboard square behind the plumb line so that the string cuts through two opposite corners. Mark all four points, then move the square down. Continue in this way to make a grid for stamping a regular pattern.

Kitchens

Considering the effort and financial outlay involved
in replacing a kitchen, stamp decorating seems a particularly
attractive option when you find that you simply cannot bear
your existing kitchen any longer. Stamping allows you creative
free-rein, dependant only on your imagination and the amount
of time you have available; whether your kitchen is in need of
a complete new image or just a little vamping-up, the extent of
the changes you make is entirely up to you. Experiment with
commercial and home-made stamps, with colors and designs,
to find the look best suited to your home.

SCANDINAVIAN KITCHEN

Replacing a kitchen is one of the major financial outlays facing a homeowner,
and also a major disruption. It often involves waiting a long time for your dream kitchen
while you put up with an outdated and intensely disliked one.
This project will revitalize and update your existing kitchen so that you may well stop pining for that
renovation altogether. The most time-consuming part of the project is painting the cabinets and
walls white, but once you've done that, you can stamp on the heart pattern that really makes the
change. Don't worry if you've got formica cabinets, as they can be cleaned to remove any grease and
then painted with an oil-based matte paint such as eggshell or satinwood. If your units are white, but
very clinical, you can brighten them up by adding red wooden handles to match the hearts.
Start this project on a Saturday morning and you could have a new-look kitchen
by the end of the weekend.

YOU WILL NEED
thick cardboard
scissors
red latex paint
plate
foam roller
small and large heart stamps
paper towels
ruler
pencil
clear matte varnish and brush (optional)
red and white gingham curtains
*backing paper (such as thin cardboard or
newspaper)*
fabric paint in pink and white
iron

1 Cut a square of thick cardboard, approximately 12x12in. To stamp the top frieze, hold the cardboard square against the wall with the top edge resting against the ceiling. Assuming that the ceiling is at a right angle to the wall, this will give you a straight line to follow. Otherwise, you will need to make adjustments visually.

Spread some red paint onto the plate and run the roller through it until it is evenly coated. Ink the small stamp and begin printing in the lefthand corner. Butt the edge of the stamp block up against the cardboard square and print a close row of hearts.

2 Print the first heart in the second row with the point facing up. Align the cardboard square with the bottom of the print and hold it in place to keep a straight line along the row.

▶

3 To print the frieze above the work surface, first cut out a piece of thick cardboard the width of the desired gap between the work surface and the border. Place this against the wall, resting on the work surface, and rest the base of the stamp block on it.

Ink the large stamp with red paint and then blot it before stamping so that the print is very light and airy.

4 Ink the small stamp and print a row of upside-down hearts between the large hearts.

5 To print the cabinets, use a ruler and pencil to mark the center point of each cabinet door.

6 Ink the large stamp and print one heart above the center point and one below so that the points face inward.

7 Ink the small stamp and print a heart on either side of the center point with the points facing inward. The cabinet doors can be protected by applying a coat of varnish.

8 To print the curtains, protect your work surface with a large sheet of paper and spread the fabric over this. Put the curtains on some backing paper on a work surface.

9 Spread some pink fabric paint onto the plate and run the roller through it until it is evenly coated. Ink the small stamp and print pink hearts down the side edges with two red squares between each one.

10 Stamp pink hearts across the fabric, counting six red squares between the points on the first row. Then begin the second row six squares down and three across. Repeat these two rows to cover both the curtains.

11 Ink the large stamp with white fabric paint, then over-print all the pink hearts. Fix the fabric paint with a hot iron following the manufacturer's instructions.

HEART VALANCE

This valance coordinates nicely with the kitchen project, but you could also try it in another room. Valances add depth to windows and they are very easy to make. Attach a wooden shelf to the top of the window frame. Cut the front and side pieces from composition board and hammer them in place with panel pins. A jigsaw is useful for cutting a scalloped edge, but a straight edge looks just as good.

YOU WILL NEED
latex paint in white and red
paintbrush
plate
foam roller
trellis heart stamp

1 Paint the valance white and let dry. Spread some red paint onto the plate and run the roller through it until it is evenly coated.

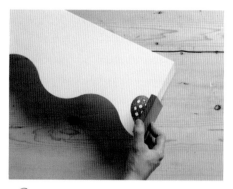

2 Ink the stamp and begin printing at one end of the front board. Use only half of the stamp for the first print so that the other half can be printed on the side piece to make the design wrap around the corner. Aim to make these prints as symmetrical as possible.

3 Stamp one heart in each scallop (if you have them); otherwise stamp them at equal distances along the length of the valance.

WINDOW BOX

Galvanized iron has staged a comeback recently and it is definitely here to stay.
Although many of the everyday objects around the home are now mass-produced in plastic,
you just can't beat the look of iron alternatives.
The individuality of the window box in this project will enhance any window ledge. The three
hearts were stamped with acrylic paint to make it just that bit more special. Plant it with flowers
and you've got a complete showpiece!

YOU WILL NEED
galvanized iron window box
ruler
pencil
red acrylic paint
plate
foam roller
small and trellis heart stamps

1 Clean the surface of the window box. Using a ruler, mark the centre point with a pencil.

2 Spread some red paint on to the plate and run the roller through it until it is evenly coated. Ink the small stamp and print a heart at the centre.

3 Ink the trellis stamp with the red paint and make a print either side of the small heart.

COUNTRY KITCHEN

Specialty stores sell beautifully decorated tiles, but they can be very expensive. So why not use stamps and paint to make your own set of custom tiles? The grape stamp is inked with two shades of green that blend in the middle in a slightly different way each time. Small touches such as the weathered hanging rail and the wooden plate add rustic authenticity to a country kitchen. The wood for the rail needs to be old and weathered. The nails banged into the rail as hangers are called "cut" nails, which are used for floorboarding. Attach the rail to the wall and hang fresh herbs from it, conveniently close to the stove. The wooden plate is stamped with different parts of the tendril motif to make a decorative border and central design.

YOU WILL NEED
plain tiles
clean cloths
acrylic enamel paint in blue-green and
yellow-green
plates
foam rollers
grape, leaf and tendril stamps
olive-green latex or acrylic paint
scrap paper
weathered piece of wood, maximum 12 in
long
long cut nails or hooks
hammer or drill
black stamp pad
scissors
wooden plate, sanded to remove any
stain or varnish
vegetable oil

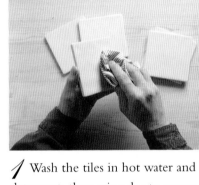

1 Wash the tiles in hot water and detergent, then wipe dry to ensure that there is no grease on the surface.

2 Spread some blue-green acrylic enamel paint onto one plate and some yellow-green onto another. Run the rollers through the paint until they are evenly coated.

3 Ink the leaf, the top and the right side of the grape stamp with the blue-green roller. Ink the rest of the stamp with the yellow-green roller.

4 Stamp a bunch of grapes in the center of each tile. Remove the stamp directly, taking care not to smudge the print. If you do make a mistake, wipe off the paint with a clean cloth and start again. Follow the manufacturer's instructions to "fire" the tiles in the oven if required.

5 For the hanging rail, spread some olive-green latex paint onto a plate and run a roller through it until it is evenly coated. Ink the leaf stamp and stamp twice onto scrap paper to remove some of the paint.

6 Stamp onto the length of weathered wood without re-inking the stamp. The resulting print will be light and faded-looking, like the wood itself. Make as many prints as you can fit along the length. Hammer in the nails or drill and screw in the hooks to complete the hanging rail.

7 For the wooden plate, stamp several tendrils onto scrap paper and cut them out. Arrange them on the plate to work out the spacing and positioning of the motifs.

8 Spread some olive-green emulsion or acrylic paint on to a plate and run the roller through it until it is evenly coated. Ink the corner of the tendril stamp comprising the two curls that will make up the border pattern and carefully begin stamping around the edge of the plate.

9 Ink the whole stamp and stamp two tendrils in the centre of the plate. Leave to dry.

10 Dip a clean cloth into some vegetable oil and rub this into the whole surface of the plate, including the stamped pattern. You can repeat this process once all the oil has been absorbed into the wood. Each time you rub oil into the plate, the colour of the wood will deepen.

COFFEE CANISTER

Rescue an old kitchen canister and give it a new identity as a piece of folk art. Painted tinware was very popular with early American settlers, and for years peddlers roamed the countryside loaded down with brightly painted cans, jugs and bowls they sold from door to door. All these years later tinware is still a popular way of brightening up kitchen shelves. Prepare this canister by rubbing down the old paint with sandpaper to provide a surface for a fresh coat of latex paint. After stamping, bring out the color and protect the surface with several coats of clear varnish.

YOU WILL NEED
empty coffee can
sandpaper
latex paint in brick-red, black and bright
red
fine artist's paintbrushes
plates
foam roller
tulip stamp
clear gloss varnish and brush

1 Rub the canister with sandpaper. Paint the canister and lid with brick-red latex paint. Leave to dry, then paint the rim of the lid black.

2 Run the roller through the black paint until it is evenly coated. Ink the tulip stamp and print a tulip on the side of the canister, tilting the stamp block around the curve of the canister.

3 Fill in the tulip using bright red paint and a fine paintbrush.

4 Apply several coats of gloss varnish to seal and protect the canister. Allow each coat to dry completely before applying the next.

VINE LEAF CUTLERY RACK

A small wooden cutlery rack like this one provides another ideal surface for stamping. Use the stamps to loosely coordinate your kitchen or dining room without being swamped by matching patterns and colors. The wood has been stained blue and the stain is then rubbed back to reveal some of the natural grain underneath. The two colors of the pattern are stamped separately using thinned latex paint for a light and airy finish.

YOU WILL NEED
wooden cutlery rack, stained blue
fine sandpaper
latex paint or acrylic paint in dark and
light olive-green
plate
foam roller
leaf stamp

1 Sand the surface of the cutlery rack to reveal some of the grain. Spread some dark olive-green paint onto a plate and thin it with water to a runny consistency.

2 Use the roller to ink the leaf stamp. Print two leaves side by side on the back and front of the rack and two leaves one above the other on the sides. Allow to dry.

3 Spread some light olive-green paint onto a plate and run the roller through it until it is evenly coated. Ink just the tips of the leaves and overprint all the darker green prints. If some of the prints are slightly off-register, this will only add to the rustic appearance of the rack.

CANDLE BOX

A long time ago, every home would have had a candle box hanging on the kitchen wall to meet the lighting needs of the household. Although rarely needed in quite the same way today, candle boxes are attractive and nostalgic design features, and add to an inviting atmosphere. Candle boxes can be bought, but are quite easy to make from five pieces of wood. The open top allows you to see when your supply is running low and the sight of the new candles is somehow reassuring.

YOU WILL NEED
wooden candle box
fine sandpaper
shellac and brush
plate
dark oak wood stain
foam roller
diamond, crown and fleur-de-lys stamps
lining brush

1 Sand away any varnish and smooth any rough edges on the box.

2 Paint the bare wood with a single coat of shellac.

3 Spread some wood stain onto a plate and run the roller through it until it is evenly coated. Ink the stamps and print a single motif on each side of the box. Print the fleur-de-lys so it will be visible above the candles. Use the lining brush to paint a thin border on all sides.

BEACH-COMBER'S STOOL

If you stumble across a small milking stool like this one, don't hesitate, just buy it! These types of stools were, and still are, used in kitchens, gardens and workshops for a whole range of tasks. Small children love to sit on them, and adults find them invaluable when shelves are just out of reach. They can be used for weeding, sketching, fishing or any activity that requires being close to the ground but not actually on it.

This thrift shop find was painted orange before being stamped with the seashore pattern. It's just the thing to sit on while peeling shrimp or cleaning mussels.

YOU WILL NEED
small wooden stool
orange latex paint
paintbrush
latex, acrylic or poster paint in deep red,
purple and pale peach
plate
foam roller
shell, seahorse and starfish stamps
matte varnish and brush

1 Paint the stool orange and let dry. Spread some deep red paint onto the plate and run the roller through it until it is evenly coated. Ink the shell stamp and make a print in the center of the stool.

2 Ink the seahorse stamp with purple paint and make a print on both sides of the shell.

3 Ink the starfish stamp with pale peach paint. Print a starfish border, overlapping the edge so that the design goes down the sides of the stool.

4 When the paint has dried, apply a coat of varnish to the stool. This will dry to a matte sheen.

PROVENÇAL KITCHEN

This kitchen is a dazzling example of contrasting colors – the effect is almost electric. Colors opposite each other in the color wheel contrast most vibrantly. You could experiment equally as well with a combination of blue and orange or red and green. If, however, these colors are just too vivid, then choose a gentler color scheme with the same stamped pattern.
The kitchen walls were color washed for a mottled, patchy background. Put some wallpaper paste in the color wash to make the job a lot easier – it also prevents too many streaks running down the walls. You can stamp your cupboards to co-ordinate with the walls.

YOU WILL NEED
latex paint in deep purple and
pale yellow
wallpaper paste (made up according to the
manufacturer's instructions)
paintbrush
plumbline
approx. 12 x 12in cardboard
pencil
plates
foam rollers
rosebud and small rose stamps
acrylic paint in red and green
clear matte varnish and brush

1 To make the color wash, mix one part deep purple latex paint with one part wallpaper paste and four parts water. Make it up in multiples of six. It is best to make more than you need. Color wash the walls. If drips occur, just pick them up with the brush and work them into the surrounding wall for a patchy, mottled effect.

2 Attach the plumbline to the ceiling, just in from the corner. Hold the cardboard square against the wall so that the string cuts diagonally through the top and bottom corners. Mark all four points with a pencil. Continue moving the square and marking points to make a grid pattern.

3 Spread some deep purple paint onto the plate and run the roller through it until it is evenly coated. Ink the stamp and print a rosebud on each pencil mark until you have covered the wall. ▶

4 If you wish to create a dropped-shadow effect, clean the stamp and spread some pale yellow paint onto the plate. Ink the stamp and print over each rosebud, moving the stamp so that it is slightly off register.

5 Continue printing over the rosebuds, judging by eye the position of the yellow prints.

6 For the cupboard doors, spread some green and red paint onto the plates and run the rollers through them until they are evenly coated. Ink the rose with red and the leaves with green. (If one color mixes with the other, just wipe it off and re-ink.) Print a rose in the top lefthand corner.

7 Print the stamp horizontally and then vertically to make a border along the edges of the door panel.

8 When you have printed around the whole panel, let the paint dry before applying a coat of varnish to protect the surface.

WOODEN WINE CRATE

Old wood usually looks best with a faded rather than freshly painted pattern. The grape design here does not detract from the crate's rustic quality because it has been stamped in a muted green, then rubbed back to blend with the existing lettering on the wood. If you are lucky enough to find a custom-made wine crate like this one, it will simply need a good scrubbing with soapy water, then be left to dry before you stamp it.

YOU WILL NEED
old wine crate or similar wooden box
scrubbing brush (optional)
olive-green latex paint
plate
foam roller
grape stamp
fine sandpaper

1 If necessary, scrub the crate well with soapy water and a scrubbing brush and leave it to dry.

2 Spread some olive-green latex paint onto a plate and run the roller through it until it is evenly coated. Ink the stamp and begin stamping a random pattern of grapes. Stamp at different angles to add variety.

3 Cover all the surfaces of the crate, overlapping the edge if the planks are too narrow to take the whole motif.

4 Leave the paint to dry, then rub the pattern with sandpaper, so that it becomes faded and blends with the original surface decoration or lettering. Rub gently and aim for a patchy, distressed appearance.

GILDED TRAY

This simple wooden tray is transformed into an item of historic grandeur with an easy gilding technique. Begin by sanding away any old paint or varnish and painting the base of the tray in black and the sides in red-ocher latex paint, applying two or three coats. The heraldic motifs make up a central panel design, and the fine outline is repeated around the edge of the tray. The tray is stamped twice, first with the red-ocher and then with gold size, which is a transparent glue used for gilding. Dutch metal leaf is then applied over the size.

YOU WILL NEED
wooden tray, prepared as above
ruler
pencil
fleur-de-lys and diamond stamps
black stamp pad
scrap paper
scissors
latex paint in black and red-ocher
plates
foam roller
thin wooden stick
lining brush
gold size and Dutch metal leaf
soft and hard paintbrushes
shellac and brush

1 Measure out and mark in pencil the six-sided central panel. Draw a border around the edge of the tray. Print eight fleurs-de-lys and five diamonds on paper and cut them out. Use them to plan your design, marking the base point of each motif in pencil on the tray. Spread some red-ocher paint onto a plate and run the roller through it until it is evenly coated. Ink the stamps and print the fleur-de-lys and diamond pattern.

2 Using the stick to support your hand, use the lining brush and the red-ocher latex paint to paint a fine line around the design, following the pencil lines of the central panel. Paint another fine line just inside the edge of the tray. If you have never used a lining brush, practice making lines on scrap paper until you are confident with the technique.

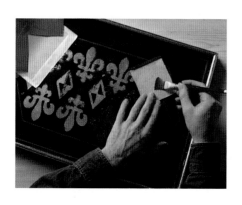

3 Paint the sides of the tray with size. Leave the size to become tacky, according to the time specified by the manufacturer. Place one sheet of Dutch metal leaf onto the size at a time and burnish with the back of a soft brush. Spread the gold size onto a plate and use the roller to ink the stamps with size. Overprint the red-ocher patterns, stamping each print slightly down and to the left of the already printed motif to create a dropped shadow effect. Leave the size to become tacky and gild with Dutch metal leaf in the same way as before. Use a stiff brush to sweep away the excess leaf. Seal the whole tray with a protective coat of shellac.

$\mathcal{B}$ATHROOMS

THE BATHROOM IS OFTEN OVERLOOKED WHEN IT COMES TO HOME-DECORATING

BUT IN FACT THIS IS ONE OF THE ROOMS THAT BENEFITS THE MOST FROM

A THOROUGH BRIGHTENING-UP. A COMPLETE NEW IMAGE IS OFTEN

WHAT IS NEEDED HERE, AND BECAUSE BATHROOMS ARE USUALLY ONE OF THE

SMALLER ROOMS IN THE HOUSE, YOU CAN AFFORD TO BE THAT LITTLE BIT

MORE ADVENTUROUS. A CRITICAL LOOK AT YOUR BATHROOM WILL SHOW

YOU WHERE IMPROVEMENTS CAN BE MADE — FEATURES TO BE HIGHLIGHTED

AND PROBLEM AREAS TO BE DISGUISED. THE GREAT BONUS OF STAMPING IS

THAT YOU CAN PRINT ON ALMOST ANY SURFACE, MAKING IT INCREDIBLY

EASY TO BUILD A THEME AND ENTIRELY CHANGE THE FEEL OF YOUR BATHROOM.

Star-studded Bathroom

Transform your bathroom into one fit for royalty or Hollywood stars in the space of a weekend.
The cost is minimal and the luxurious result is bound to impress all future bathers.
If you have an old bathroom with a boxed-in tub, it is worth investigating the underside – you
may be lucky enough to discover an old claw-footed iron tub like this one. However, the lack of
an elegant tub just adds to the challenge. You can paint the boarding and arrange it with drapes to
soften the edges.
Who could fail to feel pampered in such wonderful surroundings?

You will need
tape measure
small semicircular wooden shelf
pelform (see step 1)
craft knife
ruler
pencil
piece of calico (see step 3)
gold fabric paint or white glue mixed with
bronze powder
plate
foam roller
large star stamp
gold tassels
white glue or needle and matching
sewing threads
length of cheesecloth, for the curtains
iron-on hem tape
iron-on header tape
iron
backing paper (such as thin cardboard
or newspaper)
staple gun and staples
thumbtacks
round satin cushion
metal primer (optional)
paintbrush
cream enamel or latex paint

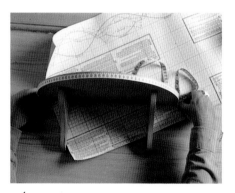

1 To make the valance, measure the curved edge of the shelf and cut the pelform to this length.

2 Using a ruler and pencil, draw a series of points along the bottom of the pelform. Cut them out.

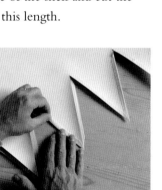

3 Place the pelform over a rectangle of calico and cut around the shape, leaving a 1¼in seam allowance. Peel off the backing paper and smooth the fabric onto the pelform. Turn the piece over and snip into the corners. Then peel off the backing strip and stick the seams down.

4 Spread some gold fabric paint onto the plate and run the roller through it until it is evenly coated. Ink the stamp and print a row of stars across the middle of the valance. Glue or sew a tassel to each point. Now fix the shelf to the wall, about 12in from the ceiling, exactly halfway along the length of the tub. ▶

5 To make the curtains, cut the cheesecloth into two pieces and turn up a seam at both ends using iron-on hem tape. Attach iron-on header tape to one end of each curtain. Lay out one of the curtains on backing paper. Spread some gold fabric paint onto the plate and run the roller through it until it is evenly coated. Ink the stamp and print a widely spaced row of stars across the bottom of the fabric.

6 Print another row of stars to fall between the stars in the first row. Repeat these rows to cover the curtain. Stamp the second curtain in the same way.

7 Gather up the curtains by pulling the header tape string. Staple the curtains to the shelf.

8 Attach the valance to the shelf using thumbtacks.

9 To make the cushion, place a ruler diagonally across the cushion and make a small pencil mark in the center. Check the position by intersecting the center point from a different angle.

10 Spread some gold fabric paint on to the plate and run the roller through it until it is evenly coated. Ink the stamp and print a single star in the center of the cushion.

11 Paint the tub with a coat of metal primer, if necessary. Paint the tub or tub panel cream and let dry. Paint the legs gold. Spread some gold fabric paint on to the plate and run the roller through it until it is evenly coated. Ink the large stamp and begin by printing the top row of stars. Continue stamping in the same way as for the curtains so that the stars fall between the spaces of the row above. Follow the curve of the tub.

REGAL BATHROOM

Decorating a bathroom on a budget usually means that all your money goes on the bathroom suite, flooring and faucets. A pure white bathroom may look clean and fresh, but a certain amount of warmth in pattern and color is needed to prevent it from seeming too clinical. Stamping enables you to achieve a coordinated finish on tiles, fabric and furniture at little extra cost. If you stamp a set of tiles using acrylic enamel paint before fixing them to the wall, the design can be baked in the oven for a very hard-wearing finish. If the tiles are already in place, you can use the same paint but it won't stand up to abrasive cleaning, so use it away from sinks and bath tubs.

YOU WILL NEED
masking tape
diamond and crown stamps
pencil
latex paint in gray and yellow-ocher
plates
foam rollers
wooden shelf with rail
white glue
clear matte varnish and brush
black stamp pad
scrap paper
scissors
white cotton piqué handtowels
gray fabric paint
iron
plain white tiles
clean cloth
grey acrylic enamel paint

1 Adhere a length of masking tape along the top edge of the the molding above the tiles or along the top of the tiles themselves if there is no molding. This will give you a straight line to stamp along. Mark the position of the actual stamp in pencil. on the edge of the stamp block.

2 Spread some gray latex paint onto a plate and run the roller through it until it is evenly coated. Ink the stamp and print the diamond border. Line up the pencil mark on the stamp block with the edge of the previous print so that the diamonds meet without overlapping.

3 To decorate the shelf, mix two parts yellow-ocher latex paint with one part white glue. The glue will make the paint stickier and will dry to give a bright, glazed finish.

4 Run the roller through the paint until it is evenly coated and ink the diamond stamp. The design of the pattern will depend on the shelf. Here, a diamond is printed on each plank to make evenly spaced rows.

5 Stamp a crown in the center at the top of the shelf and add a diamond on either side.

6 Seal the shelf with at least one coat of clear matte varnish.

7 Use the stamp pad to print twenty diamond motifs on paper and cut them out. Arrange them in three rows across the width of a towel, adjusting the spacing until you are happy with it.

8 Remove the top two rows of the pattern, leaving only the bottom row in place. Spread some gray fabric paint onto a plate and run the roller through it until it is evenly coated. Ink the stamp, and remove each paper diamond individually as you replace it with a stamped print.

9 Stamp the next row of the pattern with a diamond between each pair on the row below. Draw a line down the center of the back of the stamp block. Line it up with the top of the first row to help you position the second row.

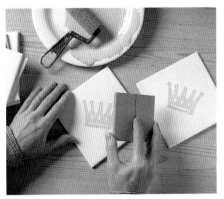

10 Complete the border pattern with a third row of diamonds. Set the fabric paint with a hot iron, according to the manufacturer's instructions.

11 Use dishwashing soap to wash the tiles, and dry them well. Hold the tiles by their edges to avoid fingerprints, which will repel the paint.

12 Spread some gray acrylic enamel paint onto a plate and run the roller through it until it is evenly coated. Ink the crown stamp and print a single crown in the center of each tile on the diagonal.

BLISSFUL BATHROOM

Sea-greens and turquoise-blues are ideal for the watery environment of a bathroom, and a floaty mood can be enhanced by the addition of colored muslin drapes or glass jars filled with bubble bath. Here, the walls are colorwashed and a cherub border is stamped on in sea-green. When the border has dried, a tinted varnish is brushed on to protect it and add another watery dimension. The chair back is stamped in latex paint and then varnished in a different shade. The plain wooden cupboard is stamped with cherubs and rubbed lightly to give it an antique look.

YOU WILL NEED
latex paint in turquoise, cream,
sea-green and pale blue
wallpaper paste
household paintbrushes
plates
foam rollers
cherub and swag stamps
pencil (optional)
level (optional)
small strip of cardboard
clear water-based varnish and brush
sepia watercolor paint
wooden kitchen chair with broad
back-rest
fine artist's paintbrush
steel wool
small wooden hall cupboard
fine-grade sandpaper
clean cloth

1 Paint the walls turquoise. Mix one part cream latex with one part wallpaper paste and four parts water. Using random brush-strokes, paint the walls. Spread some sea-green latex onto a plate and run a roller through it. Ink the first cherub stamp.

2 Rest the base of the stamp block on the top edge of the rail or tiles, or use a pencil and level to mark a line as a guide. Print a row of cherubs, alternating the two stamps and using a cardboard strip to space the border. Tint the varnish with watercolor paint and brush it over the whole wall.

3 To stamp the chair, first paint it sea-green and leave to dry. Spread some turquoise latex paint onto a plate and mix in some cream paint to lighten the shade. Run a roller through the paint until it is evenly coated. Ink the swag stamp and print a swag in the center of the chair back.

4 Lighten the sea-green paint with cream and add hand-painted detail to the stamped swag with a fine paintbrush. Allow to dry. Rub the paint with steel wool to simulate natural wear and tear. Apply a coat of clear varnish.

5 To stamp the cupboard, first paint it in pale blue latex paint. Before it has dried, rub the paint with a clean cloth so that the pale blue color stays in the grain, but the wood is revealed.

6 Rub the paint with fine-grade sandpaper to reveal some more of the wood underneath.

7 Spread some sea-green latex paint onto a plate and run the roller through it until it is evenly coated. Ink both cherub stamps and make two prints on the door panel. Allow to dry.

8 Lightly rub back the cherub stamps with a cloth to give an antique look.

$\mathcal{S}$UN-BLEACHED BATHROOM

It's hard to beat the freshness of pure, white bathroom walls, but they can look rather clinical and stark if left completely bare. This project is an ideal compromise and leaves the walls looking sun-bleached and bright.

The walls are stamped with a widely spaced pattern of yellow-ocher seashore shapes. One of the joys of stamping is creating a unique design which distinguishes your decor from ready-made wallpaper or tiles. Here the stamps are rotated with each new print to give a pleasingly random pattern.

To achieve the sun-bleached look, give the walls an all-over light wash with watered-down white latex paint. All the sharp contrasts disappear to give a calming, peaceful finish.

YOU WILL NEED
latex paint in yellow-ocher and white
plate
foam roller
shell, starfish and seahorse stamps
paintbrush
white cotton fabric, for the basin curtain
iron-on seam tape
iron
backing paper (such as thin cardboard or newspaper)
thin cardboard spacer, 1 x 6in
cobalt-blue fabric paint
curtain header tape
double-sided strong tape
unbleached calico, 1½ times the window width, plus required drop
scrap paper
eyelet kit
hammer
thick cord, 1½ times the window width

1 Spread some yellow-ocher paint onto the plate and run the roller through it until it is evenly coated. Ink the shell stamp and make a print anywhere on the wall.

2 Rotate the stamp and print a shell about two hand widths from the first one. Ink the starfish stamp and add this motif to the pattern.

3 Ink the seahorse stamp and use it to fill in the spaces to complete the pattern. Continue working until all the walls are covered.

4 Mix about six parts water with one part white latex paint and brush this wash over the entire wall to achieve the sun-bleached effect.

5 To make the basin curtain, seam all edges of the fabric using iron-on seam fix. Protect your work surface with backing paper and lay the fabric over this. Place a thin strip of cardboard along the top edge of the fabric to help space the prints for the border. Ink the seahorse stamp with cobalt-blue fabric paint and make a print at one edge with the top of the stamp butting up against the cardboard.

6 Continue stamping across the top, keeping the seahorses in a straight line and evenly spaced. If you do make a mistake, don't worry because the pleating will disguise it. Let dry.

7 Set the fabric paint with a hot iron following the manufacturer's instructions. Cut a strip of curtain header tape to fit the width of the curtain. Stick the tape to the wrong side of the curtain, along the top row of the seahorses.

8 Stick the double-sided tape along the edge of the basin, allowing enough room above it for the ruffled top of the curtain. Begin gathering the curtain by pulling the two cords.

9 If necessary, readjust the cords to make even gathers. Use the double-sided tape to secure the edge of the curtain to the basin. Work your way around the basin, so the curtain hangs evenly, with equal gathers along the width.

10 To make the window curtains, seam all edges of the fabric using iron-on seam fix. Protect your work surface with backing paper and lay the fabric over this. Ink the shell stamp with cobalt-blue fabric paint and make the first print in one corner of the curtain.

11 Rotate the stamp with each print and continue printing a random pattern. Use your hand between the shells to judge the distance between the prints.

12 Make sure that you print over the edges of the curtains in some places. Place some scrap paper under the edge of the curtain to take up the ink from the overlapping stamp. Set the fabric paint with a hot iron following the manufacturer's instructions.

13 Attach the eyelets to the top edge of the curtains, at least 4in apart.

14 Thread the cord through the eyelets from the back of the curtain to hang as shown on the right.

STARFISH BATHROOM CHAIR

Old wooden chairs are not expensive and, with a bit of careful hunting around secondhand shops, you should be able to find yourself a real bargain. Take the time to strip the old layers of paint. It might take a while, but it gives you a much better base to work on.

This chair was given an undercoat of white latex paint, then it was dragged with yellow-ocher in the direction of the grain before being stamped in light gray. Choose colors that complement your bathroom so that your Starfish Chair will blend in with existing objects.

YOU WILL NEED
medium-grade sandpaper
wooden chair
latex paint in white, yellow-ocher and
light gray
paintbrush
plate
foam roller
starfish stamp
clear matte varnish and brush

1 Sand or strip the chair, then apply a coat of white latex paint. Mix a thin wash of about five parts water to one part yellow-ocher latex paint. Use a dry brush to drag a little glaze at a time in the direction of the grain. Keep drying the brush as you work, to make sure that you do not apply too much glaze.

2 Spread some light gray paint onto the plate and run the roller through it until it is evenly coated. Ink the starfish stamp and print around the edge of the seat so that the design overlaps onto the sides.

3 Fill in the seat area with starfish stamps, rotating the stamp to a different angle after each print. Space the stamps close together to make a dense pattern. Let dry thoroughly before applying a coat of varnish to protect the surface.

Bedrooms

The great thing about decorating a bedroom is that you really

do have *carte blanche* to do whatever you like. If you feel bound by

convention with rooms that are more socially on view, you can

really let yourself go with this one — after all, this is a place of

relaxation and a room to be comfortable in. Make the look complete

with a co-ordinated scheme, by using fabric inks to stamp

a matching design on curtains, cushions and linen. Because

decorating with stamps is relatively inexpensive and hassle-free,

you can make your design as quirky as you like —

if you tire of the style, simply paint over it and stamp something new.

COTTAGE BEDROOM

Stamp denim-blue roses onto an off-white background and decorate bed linen to match. If your walls are pristine and smooth, there are ways to create the effect of rough plaster. It may seem perverse to roughen up a nice, smooth wall, but there is nothing to compare with the character of irregular plasterwork. Scratch the walls to provide a "tooth" or textured surface to work on and then apply a coat of joint compound, varying the depths in places. Let this set, then rub some of it away before it has completely hardened – this will give a deep distressed look. Use a file and coarse sandpaper to roughen up the rest of the wall, and you will have created your own cottage walls.

YOU WILL NEED
latex paint in white, buttermilk-yellow and
denim-blue
large paintbrush
plumbline
approx. 12 x 12in cardboard
pencil
plate
foam roller
large rose, rosebud and small
rose stamps
royal blue fabric paint
scrap paper
scissors
plain white sheets
iron
backing paper (such as thin cardboard or
newspaper)

1 Paint the walls white, then make a color wash by mixing four parts water to one part buttermilk-yellow paint. Brush this onto the walls, using random, sweeping strokes. If drips occur, just pick them up with the brush and work them into the wall.

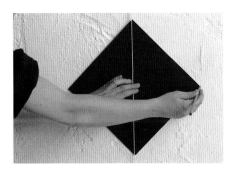

2 Hang the plumbline from the ceiling, just in from the corner. Hold the cardboard square against the wall so that the string cuts diagonally through the top and bottom corners. Mark all four points with a pencil. Continue moving the square and marking points to make a grid pattern.

3 Spread some denim-blue paint onto the plate and run the roller through it until it is evenly coated. Ink the large rose stamp and print one rose on every pencil mark.

4 Ink the rosebud stamp and print between the large roses to complete the pattern.

5 For the sheets, spread some royal-blue paint onto the plate and run the roller through it until it is evenly coated. Ink the small rose stamp and make prints on the paper. They will be used to work out the spacing.

6 Cut out the rose prints from the paper. If you do not have enough to work out a complete pattern across the sheet, print some more.

7 Wash and iron the sheet prior to stamping to ensure the best prints.

8 Place the backing paper under the ironed sheet.

9 Position the paper cutouts on the sheet, rearranging them until you are happy with the design. You could make an overall pattern of staggered rows, or simply print a border along the top.

10 Ink the stamp with the roller, and print the roses, using the paper cutouts as a guide. If you are printing a border, line up the top of the stamp block with the sewn border edge to keep the border straight.

11 Fix the fabric paint to the sheet with a hot iron following the manufacturer's instructions.

ROSE CUSHIONS

Don't get your needle and thread out for this project – just buy plain cushion covers and stamp them with contrasting colors! New cushions revitalize existing decor and they can change the mood of a room in an instant. They also cleverly distribute a thematic pattern around a room, subtly reinforcing the rosy look.

Natural fabrics like this thick cotton weave are perfect for stamping because they absorb the fabric paint easily, leaving a good, sharp print. Fabric paints can be fixed with a hot iron after applying to ensure a long-lasting and hard-wearing finish.

YOU WILL NEED
backing paper (such as thin cardboard or newspaper)
natural fabric cushion covers in two different colors
fabric paint in white and blue
plate
foam roller
rosebud, large rose and small rose stamps
scrap paper
scissors
iron

1 Place the backing paper inside the darker cushion cover. Spread some of the white paint onto the plate and run the roller through it until it is evenly coated. Ink the rosebud stamp and make the first print in the bottom righthand corner of the cover.

2 Continue stamping in rows, using the stamp block as a spacing guide – use the top edge as the position for the bottom edge of the next print. You should be able to judge the positioning by eye after a couple of prints. Fill the cover with a grid pattern of buds.

3 For the second cover, ink all three stamps with the blue paint. Stamp each one onto the scrap paper and cut them out. Use the paper patterns to work out the position of the rows.

4 Re-ink the large rose stamp and make the first print in the top lefthand corner. Use the paper pattern to help with the spacing cutouts, and complete the row.

5 Ink the small rose stamp and complete the next row, again using the paper cutouts for spacing.

6 Use the rosebud stamp in the same way to complete the pattern. Finally, fix the fabric paints on both covers with a hot iron following the paint manufacturer's instructions.

GARDEN BEDROOM

This pretty bedroom is decorated using two very quick, easy and effective techniques. First, stripes are applied onto a white wall, using the same type of small foam rubber roller as is used for inking the stamps. Rolling color on in this way gives a mottled coverage with slightly wavy edges for a subtle, faded look. The leaves are then stamped diagonally in opposite directions to make a zigzag pattern. The leaf theme is extended to the round keepsake box, which is completed with hand-painted brushstrokes.

YOU WILL NEED
wallpaper paste
latex paint in gray, leaf-green, deep blue-green, deep red and dusky pink
plates
level
2 x 1in wooden lath
masking tape
foam rollers
medium square-tipped artist's brush
leaf stamp
round, lidded wooden box
fine lining brush
clear satin varnish and brush

1 Mix the wallpaper paste according to the manufacturer's instructions, then mix one part paste with one part gray latex paint. The mixture will produce a slightly translucent glaze when dry. Tape the level to the wooden lath with masking tape.

2 Run a roller through the paint until it is evenly coated. Hold the lath in one corner of the wall and run the roller down its edge to the chair-rail or base board. Line up the ruler with the edge of this stripe and continue rolling across the wall.

3 Using a paintbrush and gray paint, complete the stripes at the ceiling and chair-rail or base board, where the roller has not reached.

4 Mix one part leaf-green latex paint with one part wallpaper paste on a plate and use to ink the leaf stamp. Stamp columns of leaves between the gray stripes. Stamp the leaves diagonally, changing the direction of the stamp to create a zigzag pattern.

5 Continue stamping until all the white stripes are filled. Re-ink the stamp when the print becomes very pale, but do allow some variety in the depth of color of the prints. This irregularity will emphasize the feel of hand-blocked wallpaper.

6 For the dressing-table box, use deep blue-green latex to paint the box and lid and leave to dry. Spread some deep red paint onto a plate and run a roller through it until it is evenly coated. Ink the leaf stamp and stamp evenly spaced leaf motifs around the sides of the box.

7 Stamp two leaves in the center of the box lid, side by side and facing in opposite directions. Use the square-tipped brush to paint a border around the top edge of the lid. Paint the sides of the lid in the same color.

8 Using a fine lining brush and dusky pink latex, paint veins on the leaves and a fine line around the inside edge of the red border. Support your painting hand with your free hand as you work. You may need to practice the strokes on scrap paper first.

9 Let the paint dry, then seal the box with a coat of satin varnish.

STARRY BEDROOM

At first glance, this bedroom looks wallpapered, but a closer examination reveals the hand-printed irregularity of the star stamps – some are almost solid color while others look very faded. This effect is achieved by making several prints before re-inking the stamp. The idea is to get away from the monotony of machine-printed wallpaper, where one motif is the exact replica of the next, and create the effect of exclusive, hand-blocked wallpaper at a fraction of the price. The grid for the stars is marked using a plumbline and pencil. If you haven't got a plumbline, make your own by tying a key to a piece of string. You're bound to be delighted with the final result, and feel a great sense of achievement at having done it all yourself.

YOU WILL NEED
sandy-yellow latex or distemper paint large
paintbrush
12 x 12in cardboard
plumbline
pencil
brick-red latex paint (matchpot size)
plate
foam roller
folk-art star stamp

1 Paint the walls sandy yellow with latex or distemper. You may prefer a smooth, even finish or areas of patchy color – each will create its own distinct look.

2 Hold the cardboard square diagonally against the wall in the corner at ceiling height. Attach the plumbline at ceiling height so that the string cuts through the top and bottom corners of the square. Mark all four points in pencil. Continue moving the square and marking points to form a grid.

3 Spread some brick-red paint onto the plate and run the roller through it until it is evenly coated. Ink the stamp and print a star on every pencil mark, or line the block up against each pencil mark to find your position, whichever you find easiest.

4 Experiment with the stamp and paint to see how many prints you can make before re-inking. Don't make the contrast between the pale and dark too obvious or the eye will always be drawn to these areas.

SMALL CABINET

A popular designer's trick is to paint a piece of furniture in the same colors as the background of the room, but in reverse. This coordinates the room without being overpoweringly repetitive. A small cabinet like the one in this project is perfect for such a treatment. Don't be too precise in your stamping – a fairly rough-and-ready technique gives the most pleasing results.

YOU WILL NEED
wooden cabinet
latex paint in brick-red and yellow
paintbrush
plate
foam roller
small star stamp
fine steel wool or sandpaper
water-based matte varnish and brush

1 Paint the cabinet with a base coat of brick-red latex.

2 Spread some yellow paint onto the plate and run the roller through it until it is evenly coated. Ink the stamp and print onto the cabinet.

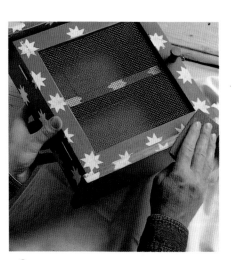

3 Rub around the edges with steel wool or sandpaper to simulate natural wear and tear. This will give an aged appearance sympathetic to a country-style interior.

4 Apply a coat of varnish tinted with the brick-red paint (one part paint to five parts varnish) to tone down the contrast between the prints and the background paint.

CHERUB BEDROOM

This bedroom has been given a complete cherubic transformation, but the use of a subtle, natural color scheme prevents the effect from being overwhelming. Earthy colors harmonize naturally to produce a restful atmosphere. The three-dimensional effect on the walls is achieved by stamping first in a darker shade and then slightly off-register in a lighter color. The cherubs seem to float free of the wall surface and even appear to be flying. The muslin drapes hang from a semi-circular shelf above the bed to make a soft frame around the pillows. The cherubs are stamped in cream fabric paint to create a very delicate pattern.

YOU WILL NEED
plumbline
10 x 10in cardboard square
pencil
latex paint in terracotta and cream
plates
foam rollers
cherub and swag stamps
11yd unbleached muslin
iron
scissors
needle and matching sewing thread
newspaper
strip of cardboard
pen
ruler
fabric paint in cream and terracotta
semicircular wooden shelf and
wall fixtures
staple gun and staples
two rough silk cushion covers
backing cardboard
black stamp pad
scrap paper
tassels
two cushion pads
vase
clean cloth
terracotta acrylic enamel paint

1 Attach a plumbline at ceiling height, just in from one corner. Hold the cardboard square against the wall so that the string cuts through the top and bottom corners. Mark all the corner points in pencil. Move the square to continue marking a grid for stamping.

2 Spread some terracotta latex paint onto a plate and run a roller through it until it is evenly coated. Use it to ink the first cherub stamp and make a print with the base of the stamp resting on one of the pencil marks. Cover the wall with cherubs, re-inking the stamp as necessary.

3 Clean and dry the stamp, then re-ink it with cream latex. Position the stamp slightly to the right and just above each terracotta cherub print to achieve a three-dimensional effect.

4 To make the drapes, wash and iron the muslin before use, then cut it into two 5½yd pieces and hem the ends. Cover a table with newspaper and lay the muslin flat.

5 Make a spacer from a long strip of cardboard, by marking lines across the strip at regular intervals. Spread some cream fabric paint onto a plate and run a roller through it until it is evenly coated. Ink the first cherub stamp and print a row across the muslin above alternate marks on the spacer.

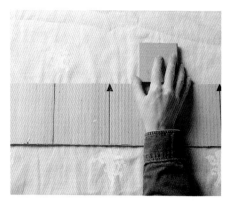

6 Print the second row of cherubs to fall between those in the first row. Use the paper strip to maintain an even distance between the rows. Move the fabric down and continue stamping to cover the whole length. Stamp the second drape in the same way. Follow the manufacturer's instructions to set the fabric paint with an iron.

7 Staple the drapes to the shelf so they meet at the front. Attach the edges first, then pleat the muslin and staple each fold to the shelf. Insert the staples vertically so they are hidden in the folds. Attach the shelf to the wall, centered above the bed and at picture rail height. Allow the drapes to fall on either side of the bed and cascade onto the floor.

8 To make the cushions, insert the backing cardboard inside the cushion covers and lay on a flat surface.

9 Use the stamp pad to print both cherub stamps on scrap paper. Arrange them on the cushion cover to plan your design.

10 Spread some terracotta fabric paint onto a plate and run a roller through it until it is evenly coated. Ink the cherub stamps and print onto the fabric, removing each paper motif as you stamp in its place. Follow the manufacturer's instructions to set the fabric paint with an iron.

11 Sew tassels onto the corners of the cushion covers and insert the cushion pads.

12 To stamp the vase, first wash it in hot water and detergent, then wipe dry with a clean cloth to ensure that there is no grease on the surface.

13 Spread some terracotta acrylic enamel paint on to a plate. Run a roller through it until it is evenly coated and ink the swag stamp.

14 Stamp swags around the vase. Remove the stamp directly and take care that it does not slide on the smooth surface and smudge the print. If you do make a mistake, wipe off the paint with a clean cloth and start again. Follow the manufacturer's instructions to "fire" the vase in a domestic oven.

BEAUTIFUL BEDROOM

Who wouldn't want to sleep in this lavender-gray and white bedroom? The choice of two cool colors has a very calming effect. The frieze is stamped in white at chair rail height around a lavender-gray wall. The simple reversal of the wall colors on the headboard provides both contrast and continuity. You can stamp on to an existing headboard or make one quite simply from a sheet of fiberboard cut to the width of the bed. Use the stamps to make matching accessories in the same colors. Make the most of the stamps' versatility by using only the central part of the tendril stamp on the narrow border of a picture frame.

YOU WILL NEED
drawing pin
string
spirit level
latex paint in white and lavender-gray
plates
foam rollers
tendril, grape and leaf stamps
headboard or sheet of fiberboard painted
white
masking tape
pencil
ruler

1 Use a drawing pin to attach one end of the string in a corner of the room at chair rail height. Run the string along the wall to the next corner and secure the end. Check the string with a spirit level and adjust if necessary.

2 Spread some white latex paint onto a plate and run a roller through it until it is evenly coated. Ink all three stamps and stamp a tendril, grape and leaf in sequence along the wall. Align the top edge of each stamp with the string and print below it.

3 When the first wall is complete, move the string to the next wall and continue all the way around the room. To decorate the headboard, stick masking tape around the top and side edges of the white board.

4 Spread some lavender-gray paint onto a plate and run a roller through it until it is evenly coated. Ink the leaf and tendril stamps. Align the stamp block with the masking tape and stamp alternate leaves and tendrils down both sides of the board.

5 Ink all three stamps and stamp a tendril, grape and leaf along the top edge of the board. Repeat the sequence to complete the row. Check the spacing before you stamp – wide spacing is better than the motifs appearing squashed together.

6 Measure a central panel on the board and lightly draw it in pencil. Stick strips of masking tape around the panel and the border. Mix some lavender-gray and white paint, then paint the border and the central panel in this pale gray color.

GRAPE JUG

A white ceramic jug like this one seems to be crying out for some stamped decoration, and the grapevine stamps do the trick in minutes. Choose a well-proportioned plain jug and transform it into something that is decorative as well as practical. Acrylic enamel paint is new on the market and, although it resembles ordinary enamel, it is in fact water-based and does not require harmful solvents for cleaning brushes and stamps. Follow the manufacturer's instructions to "fire" the stamped jug in a domestic oven to add strength and permanence to the pattern. Without "firing," the paint will only stand up to non-abrasive cleaning.

YOU WILL NEED
white ceramic jug
clean cloth
grape, tendril and leaf stamps
black stamp pad
scrap paper
scissors
acrylic enamel paint in black and ultramarine blue
plate
foam roller

1 Wash the jug in hot water and detergent, then wipe dry to ensure that there is no grease on the surface.

2 Print a grape, a tendril and a leaf on scrap paper and cut them out. Arrange them on the jug to plan the finished design.

3 Mix the black and the blue acrylic enamel paint on a plate. Run the roller through the paint until it is evenly coated and ink the stamps. Stamp the motifs following your planned arrangement as a guide.

4 The leaf may be used to fill any gaps, or the pattern may be repeated on the other side. Follow the manufacturer's instructions if you wish to make the design permanent by "firing" in the oven.

COUNTRY GRANDEUR BEDROOM

Redecorating a bedroom can be as refreshing as taking a vacation, and stamping is such fun that it won't seem like work at all. First sponge over a cream background with terracotta latex paint and add a final highlight of pink to create a warm, mottled color. Any plain light-colored wall can be covered in this way. Two of the stamps are then combined to make a border which coordinates with an all-over pattern on the wall and a bedside table. You could also decorate matching curtains and cushions, or stamp the border on sheets and pillowcases.

YOU WILL NEED
latex paint in dark salmon-pink, off-white
and dusky pink
plates
foam rollers
fleur-de-lys and diamond stamps
thin cardboard
scissors
plumbline
pencil
long ruler
small table, painted off-white
pair of compasses
black stamp pad
scrap paper
paintbrush
clear matte varnish and brush

1 Spread some dark salmon-pink latex paint onto a plate and use the roller to ink the fleur-de-lys stamp. Stamp a row of fleurs-de-lys above the chair rail using a piece of cardboard 3 inches wide to space the motifs.

2 Ink the diamond stamp with the dark salmon-pink paint, and print diamonds between the fleurs-de-lys. Use a cardboard spacing device if you are nervous about judging the positioning by eye.

3 Cut a cardboard square about 10 x 10 inches. Attach a plumbline at ceiling height, just in from one corner so that the weighted end hangs down to the border. Use to mark a grid for the diamond stamps.

4 Ink the diamond stamp with the salmon-pink paint and print a diamond on every pencil mark to make an all-over pattern.

89

5 Spread some off-white latex paint onto a plate and run the roller through it until it is evenly coated. Ink both stamps and overprint the border pattern. To create a dropped shadow effect, stamp each print slightly below and to the left of the motif that has already been printed.

6 Overprint the wall pattern in the same way.

7 Lay the ruler across the table top from corner to corner in both directions to find the central point. Mark the center lightly in pencil.

8 Set the compass to a radius of 4 inches and lightly draw a circle in the center of the table top.

9 Increase the radius to 4¾ inches. Position the point of the compass on the edge of the circle, in line with the middle of the back edge of the table. Mark the point on the circle at the other end of the compass, then move the point of the compass to this mark. Continue around the circle to make five divisions. Connect the marks with light pencil lines to make a pentagonal shape.

10 Use the stamp pad to print fifteen diamonds on paper and cut them out. Arrange them around the pentagon, as shown. Use the compass to mark the inner points of the five inward-pointing diamonds.

11 Spread some dusky pink latex paint onto a plate and run the roller through it until it is evenly coated. Ink the stamp and print the five inward-pointing diamonds at the marked positions.

12 Re-ink the stamp as necessary and print the rest of the medallion pattern. Print an arrangement of three diamonds in each corner of the table top. Paint any molding of the table in the same shade of pink. Seal the table with a coat of clear matte varnish.

PLAY ROOM

Folk art patterns really do suit all age groups, and this play room could be easily transformed into a teenager's room by removing the toys and replacing them with a desk and chair. The same bright colors appear on the walls and cushions to create a harmonious look. Dividing the wall horizontally makes the ceiling appear lower, which is ideal for a child's room. If the room has a chair-rail, paint it ocher, otherwise divide the wall with a horizontal stripe. The cushion covers can be bought or made at home. They are stamped using special fabric paint, which can be heat-sealed with an iron following the manufacturer's instructions.

YOU WILL NEED
plumb line
10 x 10in cardboard square
pencil
latex paint in gray and deep brick-red
plates
foam rollers
pineapple, leaf and tulip stamps
two yellow floor cushions or 4 yd yellow cotton fabric
iron
black stamp pad
scrap paper
scissors
fabric paint in ocher and dark brown
small pine stool or child's chair
fine sandpaper
fine artist's paintbrush
steel wool

1 Use the plumb line, cardboard square and pencil to mark a grid for stamping the pineapple motif. Spread some gray paint onto a plate and use a roller to ink the pineapple stamp. Print a pineapple on each pencil mark.

2 Wash and press the cushion covers or fabric. Stamp 12 leaves onto scrap paper, cut them out and arrange on the cushions to plan the design of the prints. Then start to print the leaf motif with fabric paint.

3 Ink the stamp with dark brown fabric paint and fill in the spaces. Use the roller to re-ink the stamp as you work, to maintain a dark color. Follow the manufacturer's instructions to seal the fabric paint with an iron.

4 Rub down the top and edges of the stool or chair with sandpaper. Use the deep brick-red paint to print two tulips, end to end, in the middle of the top of the stool. Paint a border just inside the top edge of the stool and leave to dry. Rub the paint back with steel wool to simulate wear and tear.

Nursery Walls

Children are often bombarded with a riot of primary colors or surrounded in pretty pastels, so this dark color scheme provides an unusual and refreshing change. It gives the room a wonderful period feel and the deep blue-green shade is known for its calming effect.

You can offset the dark color by painting a light color above the chair rail and laying a lighter, natural floor covering like sisal or cork tiles. The effect is rich and intense.

This idea can be adapted to any color scheme you like and you can reverse the effect by using a light background with darker stamps. Experiment with colors and shades and you'll often find that unusual combinations create the most stunning impact.

YOU WILL NEED
latex paint in deep blue-green,
sap-green and red
paintbrush
plate
foam roller
large heart stamp
water-based matte varnish and paintbrush
(optional)

1 Paint the wall below the chair rail in deep blue-green. Let dry. Spread a small amount of sap-green paint onto the plate and run the roller through it until it is evenly coated. Ink the stamp and begin printing the pattern in groups. Re-ink the stamp only when the print is very light.

2 Gradually build up the pattern all over the wall. The first prints after inking will be solid and bright; the last ones will fade into the background. This is a feature of the design, so make the most of the natural irregularities.

3 This is an optional step. If you find that the contrasts are too strong, mix some varnish with the blue-green paint (one part paint to five parts varnish) and brush it all over the pattern. Let dry.

4 Ink the stamp with red paint and over-print every third heart in the top row. Then over-print every third heart in the next row, this time starting one in from the edge. Repeat these two rows to over-print the whole pattern. Re-ink when the color has faded.

TOY BOX

This project gives instant appeal to the most ordinary of wooden boxes. It works just as well on old as new woods but, if you are using an old box, give it a good rubdown with medium- and fine-grade sandpaper before you begin. This will remove any sharp edges or splinters. The lid of the box is given a rust-red background before being stamped with three heart shapes in four colors. The stamps are rotated so that they appear at different angles and the pattern turns out quite randomly. It is best to follow the spirit of the idea rather than adhering rigidly to the instructions. That way, you will end up with a truly individual design.

YOU WILL NEED
hinged wooden chest/box with a lid
(suitable for storing toys)
rust-red latex paint
latex or acrylic paint in maroon, sap-green,
bright green and dark blue
paintbrush
plate
foam roller
small, large and trellis heart stamps
fine-grade sandpaper
matte varnish and paintbrush

1 Paint the box with rust-red paint, applying two coats to give a good matte background. Let the paint dry between coats.

2 Spread some maroon paint onto the plate and run the roller through it until it is evenly coated. Use the roller to apply a border around the edge of the lid. Let dry.

3 Spread some sap-green paint onto the plate and coat the roller. Ink the small stamp and print a few hearts randomly over the lid of the box.

4 Ink the large and the trellis stamps with the sap-green paint. Print some hearts close together and others on their own to create a random pattern. Cover the whole lid in this way.

5 Clean all three stamps and ink with the bright green paint. Build up the pattern by adding this color in the gaps, leaving enough space for the last two colors.

6 Using the dark blue paint, continue stamping the three hearts over the lid.

7 Finally, fill in the remaining background space with the maroon paint and the three heart stamps. No large spaces should remain. Let dry completely.

8 Use fine-grade sandpaper to rub down the lid where you think natural wear and tear would be the most likely to occur.

9 You can preserve the comfortable "weathered" look of the toy box by applying two coats of matte varnish.

Hallways

Your hallway and reception are the way in which you present

your home to the rest of the world and they deserve plenty of

thought and care for this reason — after all, the rooms in which

you receive your guests will undoubtedly have an effect on

their opinion of you! Stamping has to be the easiest

way to put a pattern on a wall and to make an impact

in just one weekend. Once you have mastered the basic techniques

you will begin to develop your own unique style — without any

need for great artistic talent. Build your designs around a theme

and you are sure to make a lasting impression.

TERRACOTTA ENTRANCE HALL

Corridors, entrance halls and landings are good for "sudden inspiration" decorating jobs, as they usually contain little or no furniture to be moved. Make the most of these inviting spaces by using warm colors and all-over patterns. Here, the woodwork, table and chair are all painted a pale robin's-egg blue, which is also used to stamp the leaf pattern on the semi-transparent blind. You can use fabric paint on the blind, but it is not absolutely essential, as blinds are unlikely to be washed. A painted border in the same color as the tulips adds a finishing touch to the walls, and small decorative objects such as the sconce can be stamped in similar shades.

YOU WILL NEED
latex paint in terracotta, deep plum and
gray-green
large and small paintbrushes
plumb line
10 x 10in cardboard square
pencil
plates
foam rollers
tulip and leaf stamps
ruler
masking tape (optional)
scrap paper
black stamp pad
scissors
white, semi-transparent roller blind
newspaper
robin's-egg blue latex paint
or fabric paint
iron (optional)
tin sconce
fine artist's paintbrush

1 Paint the walls terracotta and let dry. Attach the plumb line at ceiling height. Hold the cardboard square against the wall so that the string cuts through the top and bottom corners of the square. Mark all four points in pencil. Continue moving the square and marking the points to form a grid.

2 Spread some deep plum latex paint onto a plate and run a roller through it until it is evenly coated. Ink the tulip stamp and, holding it on the diagonal, make a print on each pencil mark. Position the stamp just above or just below the mark each time to create a regular pattern.

3 Change the angle of the stamp from right to left with each alternate print to give the pattern a hand-printed rather than a machine-printed look. Continue stamping tulips until the whole wall is covered.

4 Draw a line around the window a ruler's width away from the edge of the window frame. Use masking tape to make a guide-line if you don't think you will be able to paint a straight line on your own.

5 Using a small paintbrush, paint a deep plum border between the edge of the window frame and the pencil line.

6 For the blind, use the stamp pad to print 16 leaves on scrap paper. Cut them out. Lay the blind on newspaper and arrange the leaves to plan the design, starting at the bottom edge.

7 Spread some robin's-egg blue latex or fabric paint onto a plate and run a roller through it until it is evenly coated. Ink the leaf stamp and remove one paper shape at a time to stamp a leaf in its place.

8 As you complete each row, move the paper patterns up to make the next row, keeping the spacing consistent.

9 Continue in this way until the whole blind is covered. If you are using fabric paint, follow the manufacturer's instructions to seal the paint with an iron.

10 For the sconce, spread some deep plum latex paint on to a plate and run a roller through it until it is evenly coated. Ink the tulip stamp and stamp one print on the back panel of the sconce.

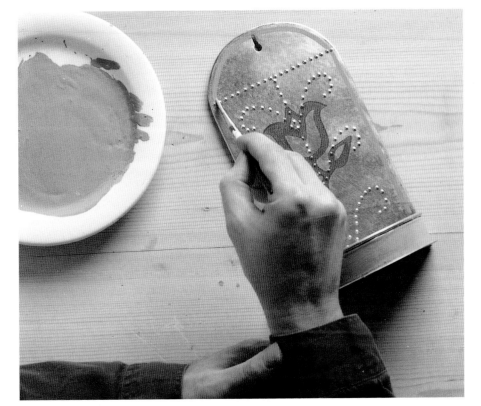

11 Use a fine artist's paintbrush to paint a gray-green line around the back panel and a thick stripe across the front.

$\mathscr{S}$TRIPED HALLWAY

All too often, creative decorating is restricted to the larger rooms of a house, but the foyer is the first thing everybody sees when they come through the front door. Why not use stamping to make a stunning first impression on your visitors?

The color scheme combines two earth colors with bright silver stars to give a slightly Moroccan feel. If you have an immovable carpet or tiles that don't suit these shades, then choose a color from your existing floor covering to highlight the walls. Foyers seldom have windows to give natural light and the inclination is to use light, bright colors to prevent them from looking gloomy. A better idea is to go for intense, dramatic colors with good electric lighting – they will turn a corridor into a welcoming foyer.

YOU WILL NEED
household sponge
latex paint in light coffee and
spicy brown
pencil
plumbline
reusable adhesive
straight-edged cardboard or wooden board,
the width required for the stamps
paintbrush
scissors
silver acrylic paint
plate
foam roller
starburst stamp

1 Use a household sponge to apply irregular patches of light coffee latex paint to the wall. Let dry.

2 Attach a plumbline at ceiling height with reusable adhesive so it hangs just away from the wall. Line up one straight edge of the cardboard or wooden board and use this as a guide to draw a straight line in pencil down the wall.

3 Move the cardboard marker one width space along the wall, and continue to mark evenly spaced lines.

4 Paint the first stripe spicy brown. Try to keep within the pencil lines, but don't worry too much about slight mistakes as the wall should look hand-painted and not have the total regularity of wallpaper.

5 Continue painting each alternate stripe, keeping within the pencil lines, but attempting to create a slightly irregular finish.

6 Cut the cardboard spacer to the length required to use as a positional guide for the stars. Spread some silver paint onto the plate and run the roller through it until it is evenly coated. Ink the stamp and print a star in each of

the spicy brown stripes along the wall, above and below the spacer. Continue printing across the wall, then return to the first stripe and start printing again, one space below the lowest star. ▷

7 Using the spacer as before, print
the first two rows of stars in the
coffee-colored stripes. Position these
stars so they fall midway between the
stars in the spicy brown stripe.

8 Continue this process to fill in the
remaining stars all down the coffee-
colored stripes.

Tuscan Hallway

All three stamps are used in this project to transform a dull space into a wall frieze that you will want to preserve forever. The finished wall will bring a touch of Tuscany into your home, even when the sky is a gloomy grey outside. The wall is divided with a strong burgundy red below and a warm cream above to visually lower the ceiling. The vine leaf pattern has been stamped on to a grid of pencil marks that is simple to measure out using a square of card and a plumbline. The lines are hand-painted using a wooden batten as a hand rest but you could also stick parallel strips of masking tape around the walls and fill in the stripes between.

You will need
tape measure
pencil
ruler
latex paint in cream, burgundy, terracotta, white and black
large household paintbrush
wallpaper paste, mixed according to the manufacturer's instructions
plate
foam roller
grape, leaf and tendril stamps
thin strip of cardboard
long-bristled lining brush
straight-edged wooden batten, 1 yd long
plumbline
6 x 6in cardboard
square-tipped artist's paintbrush
clear gloss, matt or satin varnish and brush

1 Measure the height of a dado rail and draw a line around the wall with a ruler and pencil. Paint the wall above the line cream and the area below burgundy. Mix roughly equal amounts of wallpaper paste, burgundy and terracotta paint on a plate.

2 Run the roller through the mixture until it is evenly coated and ink the grape stamp. Align the strip of cardboard with the top of the burgundy section. Rest the base of the stamp block on the cardboard to stamp a row of grapes.

3 Ink the tendril stamp and stamp a tendril at the top of each bunch of grapes. Allow some prints to be paler than others as the paint wears off the stamp block, to give a faded and patchy effect.

4 Mix a little cream paint into some white. With the lining brush, apply highlights to the grapes and the tendrils. Let the brushstrokes vary in direction and weight to add to the hand-painted look. Support your painting hand with your free hand. ▶

5 Hold the batten just below the top edge of the burgundy section and rest your painting hand on it. Slide your hand along the batten to paint a smooth, thin line in off-white. Practice this movement first and try to relax your hand to avoid jerky lines. A slight waviness to the line will not spoil the effect. Try to avoid having to paint over the line, as a single, fresh brushstroke looks better.

6 Attach a plumbline above chair rail height, just in from one corner and so that it hangs down to the skirting board. Place the cardboard square against the wall so that the string cuts through the top and bottom corners. Mark all the corner points in pencil.

7 Move the cardboard down so that the top corner rests on the lowest pencil mark. Complete one column of the grid in this way, then move the plumbline across and continue until the lower wall is completely covered with a grid of pencil marks.

8 Mix a small amount of black paint into the burgundy to deepen the color. Spread some dark burgundy paint onto a plate and run the roller through it until it is evenly coated. Ink the leaf stamp and make a print on one of the pencil marks.

9 Position the stamp just above or just below the pencil mark each time to create a regular pattern over the whole lower wall.

10 Move the batten about 1in down from the cream line and use the square-tipped artist's brush to paint a second, broader line. Keep the line as fresh as possible; visible brushstrokes are preferable to solid, flat color. Apply a coat of varnish to the lower wall to seal and protect the paint.

MEDIEVAL HALLWAY

Decorate your hallway using medieval patterns and colors that will make every entrance a dramatic one for you and your visitors. Hallways often seem dark and narrow but can be lightened and brightened using two colors of paint. A dark color above chair rail height creates the illusion of a lower ceiling, while a light color below, combined with a light floor covering, seems to push the walls outward to give the illusion of width. The crown pattern is then stamped on the walls in a diagonal grid that is easy to draw using a plumbline and a square of cardboard.

YOU WILL NEED
pencil
latex paint in dark blue-green, buttermilk
yellow and light cream
paintbrush
fine sandpaper
masking tape
ruler
paint roller
wallpaper paste (mixed according to the
manufacturer's instructions)
plate
foam roller
diamond and crown stamps
plumbline
square of cardboard

1 Draw a horizontal pencil line on the wall, at chair rail height. Paint the top half blue-green and the bottom buttermilk yellow. When dry, lightly sand the blue-green paint. Adhere a strip of masking tape along the lower edge of the blue-green, and another 4 inches below. Apply light cream with a dry roller over the yellow.

2 Stick another length of masking tape 5 inches below the one marking the edge of the green section. Using a paintbrush and blue-green paint, fill in the stripe between the two lower strips of tape. Leave to dry and then peel off the tape. Lightly sand the blue-green stripe so it matches the upper section of the wall.

3 On a plate, mix one part blue-green paint with two parts pre-mixed wallpaper paste and stir well. Ink the diamond stamp with the foam rubber roller and stamp a row of diamonds on the narrow cream stripe.

4 Use a plumbline and a square of cardboard to mark an all-over grid on the cream half of the wall. This will be used as a guide for the crown stamps.

5 Ink the crown stamp with the blue-green paint and wallpaper paste mixture and stamp a motif on each pencil mark. Make several prints before re-inking to create variation in the density of the prints.

GOTHIC CUPBOARD

Visit junk shops to find old pieces of furniture with interesting detailing and panels that are large enough to be stamped with a heraldic design. This small bedside cupboard looked very gloomy with its original dark surface, but refinished and stamped, it has become the unique centerpiece of the medieval entrance hall.

YOU WILL NEED
small wooden cupboard
fine sandpaper
emulsion paint in rust-brown, dark blue-green, lilac and yellow-ocher
paintbrush
medium-sized artist's paintbrush
black stamp pad
diamond and fleur-de-lys stamps
scrap paper
scissors
pencil
ruler (optional)
plates
foam rollers
red-orange, smooth-flowing water-based paint (thinned latex paint, poster paint or ready-mixed watercolor)
lining brush
shellac and brush
water-based tinted varnish
fine steel wool

1 Sand away the old varnish or paint. Paint the main body of the cupboard rust-brown and the panels and any carved details blue-green. Use the artist's brush to paint the blue-green right into the panel edges to ensure even coverage.

2 Use the stamp pad to print the diamond and fleur-de-lys motifs on paper and cut them out. Lay them on the panels to plan your pattern. Make a small pencil mark on the panel at the base point of each motif to use as a guide for stamping. Use a ruler if necessary to make sure the design is symmetrical. Mark the base point of the motif on the back of each stamp block so that you can line up the marks when you print.

3 Spread some lilac paint onto a plate and run the roller through it until it is evenly coated. Ink the diamond stamp and print diamonds using the pencil marks as a guide.

4 Spread some yellow-ocher paint onto a plate and ink the fleur-de-lys stamp. Print the fleur-de-lys designs, using the pencil marks as a guide.

5 Using red-orange paint and the lining brush, add hand-painted details to the motifs. Support your painting hand with your spare hand resting on the surface of the cupboard, and aim to get a smooth, continuous line.

6 Apply a coat of shellac to seal the surface for varnishing and allow it to dry. Apply a fairly thick coat of tinted varnish and allow it to dry. Rub the raised areas and edges of the cupboard with fine steel wool to simulate natural wear and tear.

Heavenly Hallway

The cherubs are stamped in silhouette on this hallway wall, framed in medallions of pale yellow on a dove-gray background. The yellow medallions are stenciled on to the gray background, and the combination of colors softens the potentially hard-edged, dark silhouettes. The stencil can be cut from cardboard or transparent mylar, and the paint is applied with the same roller that is used for inking the stamps. The cherubic theme is extended to the accessories.

You will need
latex paint in dove-gray, pale yellow and
charcoal-gray
household paintbrushes
plumbline
10 x 10in cardboard square
pencil
ruler
stencil cardboard
scalpel or craft knife
cutting mat
plates
foam rollers
cherub and swag stamps
wooden box with lid
fine-grade sandpaper
cloth
burnt-umber oil paint
cream fabric lampshade and ceramic lamp
base
black stamp pad
scrap paper
scissors
masking tape

1 Paint the wall dove-gray and allow to dry. Attach a plumbline at ceiling height, just in from one corner. Hold the cardboard square against the wall so that the string cuts through the top and bottom corners. Mark all the corner points in pencil. Move the cardboard and continue marking the wall to make a grid for the stamps.

2 Use a pencil and ruler to draw the medallion shape on a sheet of stencil card. Carefully cut out the stencil using a scalpel or craft knife on a cutting mat. Spread yellow latex paint onto a plate and run the roller through it until it is evenly coated.

3 Position the stencil on one of the pencil marks and use the paint-covered roller to stencil the medallion shape. Paint all the medallions in this way, positioning the stencil in the same place on each pencil mark.

4 Ink the first cherub stamp with charcoal-gray paint and make a print inside each medallion.

5 Paint the wooden box pale yellow, inside and out, and leave to dry.

6 Spread some charcoal-gray paint onto a plate and run a roller through it until it is evenly coated. Ink the second cherub stamp and make a print in the center of the box lid. Print the swag stamp directly beneath the cherub print.

7 Measure the sides of the box to determine the number of swag prints that will fit comfortably in a row. Mark the positions in pencil or judge by eye to add swags around the sides of the box. Leave to dry.

8 Rub the corners and edges of the box with fine-grade sandpaper. Rub the prints in places to add a faded, aged look. Use a cloth to rub burnt-umber artist's oil color onto the whole box, to give an antique appearance.

9 For the lampshade, stamp several swags on scrap paper and cut them out. Arrange the cut-outs on the lampshade to plan your design. Hold each piece in place with a small piece of masking tape.

10 Spread some dove-gray paint onto a plate and run a roller through it until it is evenly coated. Ink the swag stamp and print swags around the top of the lampshade, removing each paper motif before you stamp a design in its place.

11 Continue stamping around the base of the shade in the same way, removing each paper motif in turn.

12 Stamp swags around the lamp base to complete the co-ordinated look. Judge the positioning by eye, or use paper motifs as before.

ROSE HALLWAY

New homes are wonderfully fresh, but the perfectly even walls can look plain if you are used to details such as chair rails and deep baseboards. This project shows you how to retain the freshness of new pastel paintwork and add interest with a frieze at chair rail height and a coat of color wash below it.

Don't worry about painting in a straight line for the frieze – just use two strips of low-tack masking tape and paint between them. You could even try doing it freehand, as it does add character to the decoration, even if you do wobble a bit!

Wooden furniture is given a distressed paint finish in toning colors, and stamped with the rose designs to coordinate with the walls.

YOU WILL NEED
sandpaper (optional)
latex paint in cream, blue-green,
dusky-blue and peach
paintbrush
cloth
plates
foam roller
scrap paper
rosebud, small rose and large rose
stamps
tape measure
pencil
wallpaper paste (made up according
to the manufacturer's instructions)
masking tape
carpenter's level
straight-edged plank of wood
square-tipped 1in artist's brush

1 To prepare the furniture, rub each piece down with sandpaper and apply a coat of cream paint. Make the blue-green glaze by diluting one part paint with three parts water and then brush it on following the direction of the grain. Before the paint has dried, use a cloth to wipe off some of the paint.

2 Spread the dusky-blue paint onto the plate and run the roller through it. Ink the rosebud stamp and print the design onto the paper.

3 Referring to the paper pattern, stamp the design in position on your chosen piece of furniture.

4 Stamp more rosebuds on either side of the central design. Work with the shape of the furniture to decide upon the best position and the number of prints.

5 If you are decorating a desk or dresser, unscrew and remove any handles, then stamp the pattern on the drawer fronts. Screw the handles back in after the paint has dried.

6 For a small piece of furniture, like this chair, a simple design is best. Paint the chair cream-colored, then print a single small rose in peach.

7 To make the color wash for the walls, mix one part peach paint with one part wallpaper paste and four parts water. Make it up in multiples of six. It is best to make more than you need, so that you can do the whole room from the same batch to ensure a color match. Unless the room has been painted recently, apply a coat of cream latex paint to the walls.

8 Measure about 36in from the floor and make a pencil mark on the wall. Tape the carpenter's level to the plank and draw a straight line all round the room 36in above floor level. Draw another line 1¼in above it.

9 Apply the color wash below the bottom line using random sweeping brushstrokes. If drips occur, just pick them up with the brush and work them into the wall. Aim for a patchy, mottled effect.

10 If you have a steady hand, paint
the dusky-blue stripe freehand with
the square-tipped brush, otherwise use
masking tape as a guide and remove it
when the paint is dry.

11 Spread the dusky-blue and
peach paints onto the plates and use
the foam roller or paintbrush to ink
the large rose stamp, using the colors
as shown. Print with the stamp base
resting on the top of the blue stripe.
Continue all around the room, re-
inking each time for a regular print.

TUMBLING ROSE CHAIR COVER

Ready-made slipcovers for director's and wicker chairs provide an innovative way of restyling a room. It is rather like putting on a new jacket and changing your image.

The design of the roses follows the curve of the chair and the direction of the seat. One of the advantages of these covers is that you can use them to disguise less-than-perfect chairs that are still structurally sound. Look out for old chairs with sprung seats – their appearance may have been spoiled by coats of paint over the years, but they're still ideal for a slipcover.

YOU WILL NEED
fabric paint in green and red
plate
foam rollers
large rose stamp
ready-made calico slipcover
backing paper (such as thin cardboard or newspaper)
iron

1 Spread some green and red paint onto the plate and run the rollers through them until they are evenly coated. Ink the rose petals red and the stalk and leaves green.

2 Place the backing paper behind the lower front panel of the slipcover and begin stamping the roses. Rotate the stamp in your hand after each print to get the tumbling rose effect.

3 Place the backing paper behind the seat section and stamp the roses in the same way as the front.

4 Place the backing sheet inside the top section and stamp the top row, following the shape of the slip cover. Continue stamping to fill the cover, rotating the stamp as you did before. Fix the fabric paint on the chair cover with a hot iron following the manufacturer's instructions.

DETAILS & ACCESSORIES

THE ABILITY TO ACCESSORIZE AND PAY ATTENTION TO FINE DETAIL IS A

VALUABLE ASSET WHICH WILL ADD VISUAL INTEREST TO ANY ROOM AND

GIVES SUBSTANTIAL WEIGHT TO ANY THEME YOU MAY CHOOSE TO ADOPT.

THESE FINAL TOUCHES MAKE YOUR INTERIORS PARTICULAR TO YOU. THEY ARE

ALSO THE IDEAL STARTING POINT IF YOU ARE NEW TO THE IDEA OF

STAMP DECORATING. EXPERIMENT WITH COLORS AND STAMP DESIGNS ON

SHEETS OF PLAIN GIFTWRAP AND YOU WILL BE AMAZED AT HOW

GOOD THE PAPER WILL LOOK WITH EVEN THE MOST BASIC OF STAMP ARRANGEMENTS.

SEE HOW EFFECTIVE A SIMPLE, STRONG MOTIF CAN BE AND THEN START ADDING

OTHER MORE COMPLICATED DESIGNS TO YOUR COLLECTION.

CHERUB SHOPPING BAG

Large canvas shopping bags with shoulder straps are both fashionable and useful. They come in a range of plain colors that seem to cry out for an individual touch. Stamping works well on canvas, and you can choose from fabric paint, acrylics or household latex. Bear in mind that you will not be able to wash the bag if you use latex or acrylic, while fabric paint can be set with an iron to make it permanent and washable.

YOU WILL NEED
blue canvas shopping bag
backing cardboard
cherub and swag stamps
black stamp pad
scrap paper
scissors
latex, acrylic or fabric paint in white
and pale blue
plate
roller
iron (optional)

1 Lay the bag on a flat surface and insert the backing cardboard to prevent the paint from leaking through to the other side.

2 Make several cherub and swag prints on scrap paper. Cut them out and arrange them on the bag to plan your design.

3 Spread some white paint on to the plate and run the roller through it until it is evenly coated. Ink the cherub and swag stamps and print the pattern, removing each paper motif and stamping in its place. Allow to dry, then ink the edges of the stamps with pale blue paint. Over-print the white design to create a shadow effect. If using fabric paint, follow the paint manufacturer's instructions to set the design with an iron.

CUPID MUGS

Considering the range of mugs produced, it can be extraordinarily difficult to find one that has a shape, color and pattern you like. This project mixes and matches the colors and patterns of the mugs, while sticking to the same simple shape. Mugs can be successfully stamped with acrylic enamel paints and "fired" in a domestic oven to make the design permanent. Follow the manufacturer's instructions so the paint will withstand the hottest dishwasher.

YOU WILL NEED
four mugs in different colors
acrylic enamel paints in the same four colors
(or as close as possible)
four plates
foam roller
cherub stamps

1 Wash the mugs in hot water and detergent and dry thoroughly. Spread one color of acrylic enamel paint onto each of the plates. Decide which color to stamp on each mug.

2 Run the roller through one of the colors until it is evenly coated and use it to ink the stamp. Stamp the cherub on the first mug, removing the stamp directly to prevent it from sliding on the smooth surface.

3 Wash and dry the roller and stamp, then re-ink and stamp the second mug. Stamp all four mugs in this way, using both cherub stamps. Follow the manufacturer's instructions to "fire" the mugs in a domestic oven to make the design permanent.

VINTAGE GLASS BOWL

Turn a plain glass bowl into an exquisite table centerpiece by stamping a white tendril pattern on the outside. Stamped glassware looks wonderful because the opaque patterns seem to intermingle as you look through the transparent glass. Another advantage is that you can see the stamp as the print is being made, which helps you position it correctly and avoid overlaps and smudges. Glass painting has become popular recently and there are several brands of glass paint available. Acrylic enamel paint has a good consistency for stamping and is water-based, allowing you to simply wipe it off and start again if you make a mistake.

YOU WILL NEED
plain glass bowl
clean cloth
white acrylic enamel paint
plate
foam roller
tendril stamp

1 Wash the bowl in hot water and detergent, then wipe dry to ensure that there is no grease on the surface. Spread some white acrylic enamel paint onto a plate and run the roller through it until it is evenly coated.

2 Ink the tendril stamp and stamp the first row of prints around the base of the bowl. Remove the stamp directly, taking care that it does not slide or smudge the print. If you do make a mistake, wipe off the paint with a clean cloth and start again.

3 Turn the stamp the other way up to stamp the second row, positioning the prints in between the tendrils on the first row, so that there are no obvious gaps.

4 Stamp one more row with the stamp the original way up. Allow the stamp to overlap the edge of the bowl, so that most of the stem is left out. Leave the bowl to dry or "fire" it in the oven to fix the design, following the paint manufacturer's instructions.

PINEAPPLE PLACEMATS

Placemats are often overpriced in stores and the available designs are often uninspired. These placemats are cut from wood and painted a deep rich blue before being stamped and outlined in light blue. This classic color combination would suit a formal dinner setting, while using brighter colors will give a tropical look. Experiment with colors and decorate a set of mats to suit your own style of entertaining.

YOU WILL NEED
medium artist's paintbrush or lining brush
light blue latex paint
mats cut from thin wood,
painted dark blue
plate
foam roller
pineapple stamp
clear satin varnish and brush

1 Using a medium artist's paintbrush or lining brush and light blue latex, paint a line around the edge of each mat. Support your painting hand with your free hand as you work.

2 Spread some light blue paint onto a plate and run the roller through it until it is evenly coated. Ink the pineapple stamp and stamp a single print in the center of the mat.

3 Stamp an angled print on either side of the first. Seal and protect the mat with several coats of clear satin varnish, allowing each coat to dry before applying the next.

TABLE NAPKINS

These stamped table napkins look great with rush mats on a wooden tabletop. They bring together even the most casual collection of plates, glasses and cutlery to look like a deliberate choice. You can buy a set of plain table napkins or make your own by sewing straight seams along the edges of squares of cotton fabric. Stamping on fabric is easy and special fabric paints can be heat-treated with a hot iron to make the pattern permanent. Follow the manufacturer's instructions, which may vary from brand to brand.

YOU WILL NEED
terracotta-colored table napkins
iron
newspaper
cream-colored fabric paint
plate
foam roller
grape and tendril stamps

2 Stamp a bunch of grapes halfway along each edge, then ink the tendril stamp and print tendrils between the grapes. Stamp all the napkins in this way and leave to dry. Seal the design with an iron, following the paint manufacturer's instructions.

1 Wash and iron the napkins to remove any glaze that may block the paint's absorption. Lay the first napkin on top of several sheets of newspaper. Spread some cream fabric paint onto a plate and run the roller through it until it is evenly coated. Ink the grape stamp and print a bunch of grapes in each corner of the napkin.

PICTURE FRAME

This project combines all the creative possibilities of stamping. It involves four processes: painting a background, stamping in one color, over-printing in a second color and rubbing down to the wood. These processes transform a plain wooden frame and they are neither time-consuming nor expensive.

It is surprisingly difficult to find small, old frames that are broad enough to stamp. Fortunately, a wide range of basic, cheap frames can be found in craft stores.

YOU WILL NEED
picture frame
latex paint in sky-blue, red-brown
and gold
paintbrush
plate
foam roller
small and large star stamp
fine steel wool or sandpaper

1 Paint the frame sky-blue and let dry thoroughly.

2 Spread a small amount of red-brown paint onto the plate and run the roller through it until it is evenly coated. Ink the first stamp and print it in the middle of each side.

3 Using the red-brown paint, stamp a large star over each corner. Let dry thoroughly.

4 Ink the large stamp with gold and over-print the red-brown corner stars. Let dry before rubbing the frame gently with steel wool or sandpaper. Experiment with dropped shadow effects and other designs.

GOTHIC PLATE

Large china display plates look great on the wall and they don't have to be confined to country kitchen-type interiors, as demonstrated by this bold pattern. The plate used here is a large platter with a pale blue border outlined in navy blue, although the design can also be stamped on a plain plate. Use acrylic enamel paint on ceramics and glassware. It can be baked in a household oven according to the manufacturer's instructions. The resulting patterns are very hard-wearing and even seem to stand up to dishwashers and scouring pads, but the paints are recommended for display rather than food use.

YOU WILL NEED
black stamp pad
diamond and crown stamps
scrap paper
scissors
dinner plate
acrylic enamel paint in navy blue and deep orange
plates
foam rollers
ruler

1 Use the stamp pad to print eight diamond motifs and one crown on paper and cut them out. Arrange them on the plate to design the border pattern and central motif.

2 Spread some navy blue acrylic enamel paint onto a plate and run the roller through it until it is evenly coated. Ink the diamond stamp, then remove one of the paper shapes and stamp a diamond in its place.

3 Place a ruler under the plate, so that it runs centrally from the printed motif to the one opposite. Line up the stamp with the edge of the ruler to print the second motif. Print the motifs on the other two sides in the same way, then fill in the diamonds in between, judging by eye.

4 Ink the crown stamp with deep orange paint and stamp a single crown in the centre of the plate. Bake the plate in the oven, according to the manufacturer's instructions.

WEDDING ALBUM COVER

Custom-made wedding photograph albums are never as special as one you make yourself. For most of us, a wedding is the only time we are photographed professionally looking our very best, so the presentation should do the pictures justice. The album should have a solid spine, so don't choose the spiral-bound type. Visit a specialist paper dealer and discover the wonderful range of textured papers. The paper is stamped with gold size and gold leaf is laid on to it to create gleaming golden cherubs and swags. Initials or the date of the wedding add the finishing touch.

YOU WILL NEED
white textured paper
large photograph album with a solid spine
scissors or scalpel
cherub and swag stamps
black stamp pad
scrap paper
gold size
plate
foam roller
gold transfer leaf
soft cloth
soft-bristled paintbrush
gold transfer letters or fine artist's brush
(optional)

1 Lay the opened album on the sheet of paper and trim the paper to size. Allow a border round the edges to fold over the paper inside the cover.

2 Stamp several cherubs and swags on scrap paper and cut them out. Lay them out on the album cover with any initials or dates to plan your design. When you are happy with the design, use the paper cut-outs as a guide for positioning the stamps.

3 Spread some gold size on to a plate and run the roller through it until it is evenly coated. Ink the stamps with size and stamp the design on the album cover. Leave to dry for the time recommended by the manufacturer until the size becomes tacky.

4 Lay sheets of gold leaf on to the size and burnish the backing paper with a soft cloth. Remove the backing paper and brush away any excess gold leaf still clinging to the paper. Add initials and the date, if required, using gold transfer letters or paint them freehand in size and gild as before.

5 Cover the album with the decorated paper, checking that the design is positioned centrally on the front of the cover. Stick down the overlaps with double-sided tape on the inside of the cover.

BOOK COVERS AND SECRETS BOX

This project evokes another era, when time passed by more slowly and leisure had nothing to do with aerobics. Diaries and scrapbooks were kept and lovingly covered with printed papers and secret mementoes were hidden in locked wooden boxes. Recapture the spirit of a bygone age by stamping patterned papers and using them to bind sketch books, albums and diaries. Preserve the battered antiquity of an old wooden box by stamping it and lining it in muted shades of red and green, then rubbing back the paint to simulate years of wear and tear.

YOU WILL NEED
black stamp pad
tulip, leaf and pineapple stamps
scrap paper
textured paper
ready-mixed watercolor paint in deep red,
leaf-green and black
plates
long ruler
diary, photo album, or book, such as a
sketchbook
white glue
black bookbinding tape
cutting mat
craft knife
old wooden box
latex or acrylic paint in brick-red
and green
foam roller
2 x 1in wooden lath
lining brush
fine sandpaper or steel wool
furniture polish (optional)

1 For the book cover, use the stamp pad and print four tulips on scrap paper. Cut them out and arrange them in a row along the top edge of the textured paper, side by side and alternately facing up and down. Use these paper prints as a guide for stamping.

2 Spread some deep red watercolor paint onto a plate and dip the stamp into it. Lay the ruler across the paper and use to align the stamp to print the first row. Re-ink the stamp after three prints for an irregular hand-printed effect.

3 Move the ruler down the width of a stamp block for each new row. Stamp the rows so that the tulips lie between the prints in the previous row. Cover the paper completely and leave to dry. Print more paper, using the leaf and pineapple stamps and the leaf-green and black paint.

4 Cover the book with the paper, sticking down the corners with white glue. Place a strip of bookbinding tape along the spine to cover the paper edges so there is an equal width of tape on the front and back cover. Trim away the tape at the top and bottom with a craft knife. ▶

5 For the treasure chest, use the stamp pad to print some tulips and leaves on scrap paper and cut them out. Arrange them on the wooden box to plan your design, deciding which motifs will be red and which green.

6 Spread some brick-red latex or acrylic paint onto a plate and run the roller through it until it is evenly coated. Ink the stamps and remove one paper shape at a time to stamp a leaf or tulip motif in its place.

7 Ink the leaf stamp with sage-green paint and stamp green leaves on the box in the same way.

8 Place the lath along the edge of the box and use the sage-green paint and the lining brush to paint an outline around the box and corner motifs. Slide your hand along the lath to keep an even line.

9 Leave the paint to dry completely, then lightly rub the stamped prints with sandpaper or steel wool. The box can then be polished with furniture polish if desired.

SEAHORSE THROW

Throws are indispensable accessories in every home – while adding glorious
swatches of colors to any room, they also cleverly disguise any worn or stained patches.
Throws can be thick and wintry or light and airy like this one, which could also double up as a
sarong for a quick wraparound. Cotton crepe has a fine, crinkled texture, which adds volume to
the fabric and makes it drape well. Cotton or other natural fibers are the best choice as they
absorb the fabric paint easily. So, have a go at this throw and make a luxurious gold design
for your home.

YOU WILL NEED
*length of cotton crepe or a ready-made plain
throw*
*backing paper (such as thin cardboard or
newspaper)*
thumbtacks
gold fabric paint
plate
foam roller
seahorse and shell stamps
iron

1 Protect your work surface with backing paper. Lay the fabric over this and pin down.

2 Spread some gold fabric paint onto the plate and run the roller through it until it is evenly coated. Ink the seahorse stamp and make the first print in one corner.

3 Print a border along the top and bottom edges of the throw, alternating shells and seahorses.

4 Stamp widely spaced rows of seahorses between the borders, turning the stamp 180° each print. The prints in each row should fall between those of the previous row. Set the fabric paint with a hot iron following the manufacturer's instructions. Press directly down onto the fabric, making sure the fabric retains its texture.

CHRISTENING PARTY

The gift paper, cards and table setting featured in this project will all help to make a traditional christening party an unforgettable occasion. Use the cherubs to announce the baby's birth and herald the start of the celebrations. Buy a good-quality white paper for the cards. Some papers have scalloped edges, while others are textured. The choice is a personal one, and a textured surface may produce unusual stamped effects, so experiment on samples of paper. Set off the hand-printed wrapping paper with white satin ribbons and bows.

YOU WILL NEED
large white tablecloth or sheet
backing cardboard
fabric paint in bottle-green and silver
plates
foam rollers
swag and cherub stamps
iron
paper napkins in white and bottle-green
acrylic paint in bottle-green, white and blue-gray
white note-paper
scissors
ruler
pencil
water-based size
silver transfer leaf
fine steel wool
silver wrapping paper
newspaper
black stamp pad
scrap paper
small strip of cardboard

1 Lay the tablecloth or sheet on a table. Ink the swag stamp with bottle-green fabric paint and print across one corner of the cloth so that the tassels are about 1in from the edges. Stamp swags all around the edge of the cloth to create a scalloped effect.

2 Spread some silver fabric paint onto a plate and run a roller through it until it is evenly coated. Ink both cherub stamps and, alternating the two designs, make a print above every other swag.

3 Continue to stamp a widely spaced cherub pattern in the center of the cloth, alternating both stamps and rotating the direction of the prints. Follow the manufacturer's instructions to set the paint with an iron.

4 For the napkins, spread some green acrylic paint onto a plate and run a roller through it until it is evenly coated. Ink the cherub stamps and make one print on each white table napkin.

147

5 Spread some white acrylic paint onto a plate. Use a roller to ink the cherub stamps. Stamp a white cherub on each green napkin.

6 To make the cards, cut and fold the paper to the required size, which should be at least 5½ x 4½in. Draw pencil lines on the back of the stamp block to mark the mid-points on each side to help you position the stamp accurately each time. Spread some blue-gray acrylic paint onto a plate and run a roller through it until it is evenly coated. Ink the stamp and print cherubs on all the cards. Allow to dry.

7 Spread water-based size onto a plate and run a roller through it until it is evenly coated. Ink the cherub stamps with size and overprint the blue-grey prints. Allow to dry for the time recommended by the manufacturer until the size becomes tacky. Lay sheets of silver leaf onto the size and burnish the backing paper with a soft cloth.

8 Remove the backing paper and use steel wool to rub away any excess silver leaf still clinging to the paper.

9 To make the wrapping paper, lay the silver paper on some newspaper on a flat surface. Stamp several cherubs and swags on scrap paper and cut them out. Arrange the paper motifs on the silver paper to plan your design. Cut a cardboard strip as a guide to the spacing between the motifs.

10 Spread some bottle-green acrylic paint onto a plate and run a roller through it until it is evenly coated. Ink the cherub stamp and print cherubs on the silver paper. Use the cardboard strip to space the stamps evenly.

11 Ink the swag stamp with white paint and print the linking swags between the cherubs.

WRAPPING PAPER

Imagine never having to buy a sheet of wrapping paper again. Once you realize how easy it is to make stamped paper, there will be no turning back. Stamped paper not only looks great, but it costs so little that you will have lots of spare cash to spend on ribbon and trimmings.

Any plain paper can be stamped. The contrast between utilitarian brown wrapping paper and luxurious gold stars looks particularly striking, but for a more colorful paper, you could use tissue paper, which is available in a riotous assortment of colors.

Only the most exclusive and expensive types of commercial wrapping paper are hand-printed, so you can have the pleasure of stamping your own at a fraction of the cost.

---✳---

YOU WILL NEED
ruler
pencil
brown wrapping paper
acrylic paint in brown, blue, white
and cream
plate
foam roller
starburst, folk-art and small star stamps

1 Use the ruler and pencil to mark one edge of the wrapping paper at approximately 5in intervals.

2 Spread a small amount of brown paint onto the plate and run the roller through it until it is evenly coated. Ink the starburst stamp and print onto the wrapping paper, using the pencil marks as a guide for the first row and judging the next rows visually.

3 Ink the folk-art stamp with blue paint and stamp these stars between the brown stars.

4 Ink the small star stamp with white paint and fill in the centers of the blue stars.

5 Stamp cream stars along diagonal lines between the blue stars.

ANGEL T-SHIRTS

Fabric paints are very easy to use, come in a wide range of colors and can be set with a hot iron to make them washable and permanent. The cherub stamps can be used in many ways, including in the funky color combinations chosen here. Strong contrasts, complimentary shades or neon colors will all give the cherub a new image. By overprinting the cherubs slightly off-register in a second color, you can create a three-dimensional look. Wash and iron the T-shirt before printing to remove any glazes that may prevent the absorption of the fabric paint.

YOU WILL NEED
solid-colored T-shirts
backing cardboard
cherub and swag stamps
black stamp pad
scrap paper
scissors
fabric paint in various colors
plate
foam roller
ruler (optional)
iron

1 Lay a T-shirt on a flat surface and insert the backing cardboard to prevent the paint from leaking through to the other side.

2 Stamp several cherubs or cherubs and swags on scrap paper. Cut them out and arrange them on the T-shirt to plan your design.

3 Spread some fabric paint onto a plate and run the roller through it until it is evenly coated. Ink the cherub stamp and print the pattern, removing each paper motif and stamping a cherub in its place. Re-ink the stamp after each print and press down firmly with the stamp to allow the fabric paint to penetrate the fabric.

4 Use a ruler to help align the pattern if necessary. Experiment with other patterns and colors. Follow the paint manufacturer's instructions to set the design with an iron.

HERALDIC STATIONERY

Design and print a personalized set of stationery to add a touch of elegance to all your correspondence. Heraldic motifs have been used for centuries to decorate letters and secret diaries, but it is no longer necessary to live in a palace to be able to use them. This project demonstrates the variety of ways in which a single stamp can be used to produce different effects. The resulting stationery is based on a common theme but with plenty of individual flourishes. Experiment with your favorite color combinations, and try all-over or border patterns to add even more variety. Many craft stores sell special embossing powders that can be heated to produce a raised print.

YOU WILL NEED
dark blue artist's watercolor paint
plate
foam rollers
diamond, fleur-de-lys and crown stamps
brown packaging paper
craft knife
cutting mat
small notebook, folder, postcards and
textured and plain notepaper
gold paint
dark blue paper
ruler
T-square
white glue
fine artist's brush

1 Spread some dark blue watercolor paint onto a plate and run the roller through it until it is evenly coated. Ink the diamond stamp and print one motif onto a small piece of the brown packaging paper.

2 Cut out the diamond shape with a craft knife on a cutting mat. Try not to overcut the corners because the shape will be used as a stencil and the paint may bleed through.

3 Position the paper stencil in the middle of the notebook cover and use the roller to apply blue watercolor paint through it. Allow to dry.

4 Spread some gold paint onto a plate and run the roller through it until it is evenly coated. Ink the diamond stamp and stamp a gold print directly over the solid blue diamond, lining up the edges as closely as possible.

5 Cut a rectangle the size of the fleur-de-lys stamp block out of dark blue paper. Measure and divide it in half lengthways. Cut away one side, with a craft knife, leaving a narrow border around the edge to make a window in one side.

6 Using a ruler and T-square to position the stamp, print a dark blue fleur-de-lys in the center of the folder. Glue the blue paper over the print so that half the fleur-de-lys shows through the window.

7 Ink the fleur-de-lys stamp with gold paint. Cover the cut-out side of the design with a straight-edged piece of brown packaging paper. Stamp a gold fleur-de-lys to align with the sides of the blue print. Remove the piece of packaging paper to reveal the final design, which will be half gold and half blue.

8 Stamp a blue fleur-de-lys on a notebook cover or postcard. Cover one half of it with a straight-edged piece of packaging paper and overprint in gold to make a two-color print.

9 Fold a piece of textured notepaper
to make a card. Stamp a blue fleur-de-
lys on the front of the card. The
texture of the paper will show through
in places. Add flourishes of gold paint
using a fine artist's brush.

10 Stamp a gold crown at the top
of plain white sheets of notepaper.

SUPPLIERS

The following companies supply a wide range of stamps. If you are unable to find
the designs you like, it is sometimes possible to have them made up.

All Night Media Inc
PO Box 10607
San Rafael
CA 94912
tel: (415) 459 3013

Arthur Brown and Bro Inc
PO Box 7820
Maspeth
NY 11378
tel: (718) 628 0600

Dick Blick
PO Box 1267
Galesburg
IL 61402
tel: (309) 343 6181

Graphic Rubber Stamp Co
11250 Magnolia Blvd
North Hollywood
CA 91601
tel: (818) 762 9443

Inkadinkado
76 South Street
Boston
MA 02111
tel: (617) 338 2600

Pearl Paint Company Inc
308 Canal Street
New York
NY 10013
tel: (212) 431 7932

Posh Impressions
875 East Birch Street
Brea
CA 92621
tel: (714) 529 9933

Ranger Industries
Tinton Falls
New Jersey 07724

Rubber Stampede
PO Box 246
Berkeley
CA 94701
tel: (415) 843 8910

INDEX